PICK YOUR BRAINS
about
SCOTLAND

Mandy Kirkby

Illustrations by
Caspar Williams & Craig Dixon

CADOGAN

Acknowledgements

The author and the publisher would like to thank 'guest editors'
Annie Young (aged 13) and Clementine Hart-Walsh (aged 9).

Published by Cadogan Guides 2005

Illustrations by Caspar Williams and Craig Dixon
Illustrations and map copyright © Cadogan Guides 2005
Map by ⓉⓌ

Cadogan Guides
Network House, 1 Ariel Way, London W12 7SL
info@cadoganguides.co.uk
www.cadoganguides.com

The Globe Pequot Press
246 Goose Lane, PO Box 480, Guilford,
Connecticut 06437–0480

Design and typesetting by Mathew Lyons
Printed in Italy by Legoprint

A catalogue record for this book is available
from the British Library
ISBN 1-86011-223-4

Contents

Not to scale!

Vital Facts and Figures

Area: 78,789 square km (30,420 square miles). Scotland is the second largest of the countries that make up the United Kingdom. From north to south, it is 440 km (275 miles) long and, at its narrowest, 145 km (90 miles) wide: at that point it would take you only about two hours to drive from east to west assuming you could drive in a straight line and not hit any traffic jams (but Scottish roads tend to be wiggly and not that fast).

Population: just over 5 million. Most people live in the central region and in the towns and cities along the east coast. Only 10 per cent of the population live in the mountainous Highlands, and yet this region covers nearly two-thirds of the country.

Capital: Edinburgh. It has been the capital since about 1500. It's built around a series of extinct volcanoes and a drained loch – features that give the city a dramatic appearance. In the 19th century Edinburgh was given the nickname 'Auld Reekie' because of the clouds of smoke and the terrible smells that hung over the city.

Major cities: Glasgow (the largest city), Aberdeen, Dundee, Stirling, Inverness and Perth.

Distances: Edinburgh to London = 535 km (332 miles).
Edinburgh to Dublin = 343 km (213 miles).
Edinburgh to New York = 5,259 km (3,268 miles).

Borders: Scotland shares a border with England, but no passport is necessary! The border runs alongside a stretch of the River Tweed, over the Cheviot Hills, through Kielder Forest and down into the Solway Firth. The first border between England and Scotland was Hadrian's Wall, built by the Romans in AD 122. The Wall was much further south than the present-day border.

Regions: Aberdeen, Aberdeenshire, Angus, Argyll and Bute, Ayrshire (divided into East, North and South Ayrshire), Borders, Clackmannanshire, Dumfries and Galloway, Dundee, Dunbartonshire (East and West), Edinburgh, Falkirk, Fife, Glasgow, Highland, Inverclyde, Lanarkshire (North and South), Lothian (East, Mid and West), Moray, Orkney Islands, Perth and Kinross, Renfrewshire (one bit is plain Renfrewshire, but East Renfrewshire is separate), Shetland Islands, Stirling, Western Isles.

Flag: the Saltire. A white diagonal cross on a blue background, this represents St Andrew, the patron saint of Scotland. The Lion Rampant flag is also associated with Scotland. This shows a red lion on a golden-yellow background and is thought to come from an ancient Scottish king's coat of arms.

The purple thistle is one of Scotland's most famous emblems. The legend of the thistle goes back hundreds of years to when the Vikings invaded Scotland. A Viking raiding party was advancing in the middle of the night when one of them trod on a prickly thistle and let out a yell. The noise woke up the Scots in time to prepare for battle.

Currency: sterling. The same currency is used throughout the United Kingdom although Scotland issues its own banknotes through the Royal Bank of Scotland, the Bank of

It is estimated that there are more than 25 million people of Scottish origin living abroad, especially in the USA. For many people whose grandparents and great-grandparents left Scotland for a better way of life, tracing their ancestors' roots is popular, and thousands of Americans, Canadians, Australians and many other nationalities visit Scotland every year to see where their family originated. Where better to start than with a place name? As Scots emigrated round the world, they reminded themselves of home by giving Scottish names to the areas where they settled.

Did you know...

☞ There are 14 Aberdeens and 19 Glasgows in the USA.

☞ Bannockburn is a suburb of Brisbane in Australia and you can visit two Cullodens in the USA and two in Canada.

☞ There's a Dundee Island in Antarctica and a Dundee Beach in Australia.

☞ In Natal in South Africa, Dundee is right next door to Glencoe.

☞ You'll find three Stirlings in Canada, and a Mount Sterling in Kentucky, USA. Mount Sterling was originally spelt 'Stirling' after the Scot who founded it, but over the years, the name was mis-spelt and it's stuck.

☞ One of the most important cities in Australia is called Perth.

☞ Dunedin in New Zealand is named after Duneidin, the old word for Edinburgh.

Scotland and the Clydesdale Bank. The three banks agreed on the same colour scheme for notes of the same value, but the designs are different. Only the Royal Bank produces a £1 note. The banknotes can be used in England and Wales, although you hardly ever see them outside Scotland.

Internet domain: uk

Languages: Scots, Gaelic, English. Most of the time, you'll hear English being spoken with a Scottish accent, but additional words and phrases from the Scots language will be used. Only 1 per cent of the population use Gaelic in their everyday speech and you'll probably only hear it if you travel to some of the islands, especially the Hebrides. It is an ancient language and great efforts are made to encourage more people to use it. It's taught in schools, and programmes in Gaelic – including cookery, travel, quiz shows and children's dramas – are broadcast on television and on the radio. You can even watch Gaelic versions of *Rugrats* and *Postman Pat* (in Gaelic, he's known as *Pàdraig Post*). Many road signs and place names are written in both English and Gaelic.

Geography: Scotland is one of the last, great unspoilt wildernesses in the world. Apart from the mainland there are hundreds of islands of varying sizes, some big enough to contain their own mountain ranges.

You can divide Scotland up into three main chunks:

The Southern Uplands – this is the area south of Edinburgh and Glasgow down to the border with England. It consists of lush green valleys, farmland and ranges of hills, some very bleak and high such as the Pentlands and the Lammermuirs.

The Central Lowlands – most Scots live here, mainly in Glasgow and Edinburgh, and most of Scotland's industry is in this low-lying area of towns, cities and gentle hills.

The Highlands and Islands – the most dramatic and rugged scenery in Scotland is in this region. High mountains, deep lochs, heather-covered moorland, peat bogs and great forests. Along the northeast coast there is fertile farming land. A 100-km (60-mile) long geological fault called the Great Glen runs east to west and splits the Highlands in two.

Coastline: Scotland is surrounded by the waters of the North Sea and the Atlantic Ocean. The coastline is very rugged and has so many bays and inlets that it is estimated to be 10,000 km (6,214 miles) long. The highest cliffs in Britain are in Scotland – the Clo Mor cliffs at Cape Wrath in the far north – and they are a scary 161 m (523 ft). Large numbers of dolphins, whales and porpoises live around the Scottish coast.

Mountains: the major mountain ranges are on the mainland: the Grampians, the Cairngorms and Wester and Easter Ross but the Cuillin Mountains on the island of Skye are spectacular and are horribly difficult to climb. The highest mountain in Scotland (and in Great Britain too) is Ben Nevis in the Grampian mountains at 1,344 m (4,409 ft).

Lochs: seawater and freshwater lochs (the Scottish word for 'lakes') – are a major feature of the Highlands. The largest is Loch Ness. It is 39 km (24 miles) long and 245 m (800 ft) deep. But the deepest is

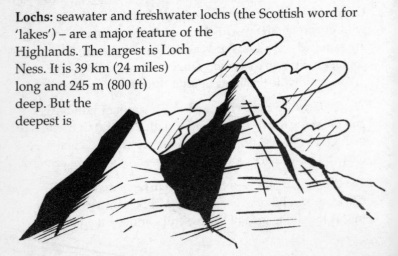

12

Loch Morar which is 328 m (1077 ft) deep.

Rivers: Scotland's major rivers are the Tay, the Spey (the fastest-flowing in the whole of Britain), the Clyde, the Tweed and the Dee.

Houses: there are a huge variety of house types in Scotland, often built with the local stone. Aberdeen, for example, is known as the 'Granite City' because many of its imposing buildings are made from local grey granite. There are two out-of-the-ordinary types of housing you should look out for – tenements and croft houses.

Tenements are mostly found in Glasgow and are blocks of red-sandstone flats, built in the 19th and early 20th centuries. The blocks are only a few storeys high and were originally designed to squeeze in as many people as possible – many families occupied flats of only two rooms. They're fascinating buildings, very solid and sturdy, and the entrances are often decorated with colourful tiles. Nowadays they're considered trendy places to live in, and people will pay quite a lot of money to do so.

Croft houses are found all over the Highlands and Islands. These cottages (many are very old) have land attached, sometimes enough to keep cows and sheep, a little like a small farm, although many of the crofters who live here have other jobs as well. You might also spot slabs of peat piled up outside the house, which are dried and then burnt as fuel. The crofter's land is rented from the local landowner and this tradition is centuries old, going back to the time when Highlanders belonged to groups called clans and the clan chief would have owned the land. At one time, it was easy for landowners to get rid of their tenants, but it's far more difficult now because there are plenty of laws to protect them.

Climate: for many months of the year, Scotland can be a chilly, misty and wet place – it's a northern European country, so what else can you expect? But if you travel west from Edinburgh you'll reach Canada, and if you go east you'll find Russia, and yet Scotland doesn't have anything like the harsh winters that these countries have to endure. This is because of Scotland's geographical position – it has the Atlantic flowing alongside its west coast, which brings warm ocean currents from the Caribbean. The whole of Scotland benefits from this general warming up, although it starts to cool down a little the further east you go. The west rarely sees frost (in fact, it's so frost-free that some botanic gardens here can grow tropical plants and trees). Mind you, Scotland is still a chilly place, but if it wasn't for the kind Atlantic Ocean, there might be

polar bears and penguins.

In the mountainous parts of Scotland the winter *can* be very cold, with blizzards and fierce winds, and there's often enough snow to go skiing. There's snow on the mountain tops for many months of the year. The lowest temperature ever recorded in Scotland was at Braemar in Aberdeenshire – a very chilly $-27.2°C$ in 1895 and 1982. The record was nearly broken again in 1995 when the temperature fell to $-27°C$.

Scottish summers are warm but rarely blistering hot, and can often keep you guessing as to what's going to happen next. So when you go out take everything with you – swimming togs, jumper, umbrella, winter coat. In fact, the weather is unpredictable all year round, so much so that people say 'If you don't like the weather, wait five minutes'. The highest summer temperature recorded was $32.8°C$ in 1933 and 1976.

If you find yourself moaning about the Scottish weather, just think that Scotland wouldn't be as beautiful a country without all that rain to keep it green and lush and full of fast-flowing rivers. And one great thing: because the country is so far north, this means that in the summer it doesn't get dark until midnight. That's a bit weird, but great fun.

Media: British national newspapers, radio and television are all available in Scotland as they cover all areas of Britain, but many Scots tend to read Scottish newspapers, listen to BBC Scotland and local radio and – though to a lesser extent – watch Scottish television. *The Scotsman* and *The Herald* are very important newspapers but rather serious, so you might like to read the *Sunday Post* which is good fun. There are lots of Scottish radio stations and television channels, and many of them make Gaelic programmes.

Travelling: in the populated areas, travelling is easy (and there's an Underground in Glasgow), but once you get into the countryside, especially the Highlands and Islands, it starts to get a bit tricky if you don't have a car. In which case, a fun way to get around is by Royal Mail Postbus. This is a mail van-cum-minibus which will transport you, plus letters and parcels, to anywhere on the van's route. You do have to pay, but you can wave at the bus to stop it at any point and catch a ride.

Highland roads can be exciting to travel along – many are just single-track and

they can take you through spectacular scenery, round the edges of great lochs and along the side of mountains. But because it's so difficult to build roads in such a mountainous regions, there really aren't very many of them. It is even more difficult to build railway lines outside the lowland region, but – just like the roads – almost any railway journey in the Highlands will take you through breathtaking scenery, and the West Highland line from Fort William to Mallaig is famous for its amazing views.

Ferries are crucial for getting to the islands and for travelling between them, although the larger ones do have airports. Ferry trips to the more remote islands can take several hours. There are very few roads on the islands and the absence of cars can feel very strange indeed.

Scottish History in a Nutshell

People first came to live in Scotland about 10,000 years ago, arriving by boat and on foot from England and Europe. At that time, most of the country would have been covered with trees, with very little wide-open space. They hunted animals and ate fruit and berries from the forest. It took thousands of years for these primitive people to clear the woodland to grow crops, to learn how to look after farm animals and to organize themselves into communities and tribes.

When the Romans invaded Scotland from England in AD 80, they faced some very hostile opponents. Thousands of years of living in a cold and mountainous environment had

---

You can see Ancient Scotland at:

☞ The Standing Stones of Callanish on the Island of Lewis where, more than 4,000 years ago, ancient Callanish man arranged more than 50 huge stones into circles and rows. It is one of the most important historical sites in the world, older than Stonehenge, although nobody is really sure why it was built.

☞ Well, only a few places because they didn't get very far, but at Bonnybridge near Stirling, you can see traces of the Antonine Wall, which – for a little while – marked the Roman border between Scotland and England. The wall is 60 km (35 miles) long, made from piled-up earth with a ditch running alongside. Archaeologists found several stones by the wall, and one which said, in Latin, 'The second Augustan Legion made this'.

toughened up the ancient people of Scotland and they outwitted the Romans time and time again. The Romans gave them the nickname 'Picts', meaning 'painted people' – probably because they tattooed their bodies. Despite thinking themselves far superior, the Romans ultimately failed to conquer the Picts and their land, and retreated back to England.

By the time the Romans abandoned Scotland completely in AD 450, the powerful Picts had gained some rivals – one tribe called the Britons, another called the Angles, another called the Scots (who would eventually give Scotland its name) and, some 250 years later, the Vikings. The Vikings were from Norway (only a few hundred kilometres/miles away across the North Sea) and had conquered the islands in the north – Shetland and Orkney. For centuries, that northernmost

St Andrews BC

part of Scotland was ruled by Norway.

Eventually all the tribes, apart from the Vikings, united in AD 843 under one ruler. They needed to stick together to keep away the English who wanted to take over Scotland. For the next 500 years, the Scottish people would have to go to war over and over again for the right to rule themselves, and many brave men such as Robert the Bruce and William Wallace became great heroes by defending Scotland and fighting for its independence.

Amid the turmoil, there had been some quiet moments, and Christianity had come to Scotland from Ireland, brought by Saint Columba. Great monasteries and magnificent churches had been established, but the thought of battle was seldom far away and the castle builders were never out of work. Scotland began to look outwards to trade its wool, coal, salt and salmon with other countries. Adventurous merchants set up trading links with Norway, Sweden, Denmark, Poland and the Netherlands. These influences can be seen in some of Edinburgh's buildings in the Old Town which don't look typically Scottish (or even English), but more like the buildings you'd find in Copenhagen or Bruges.

By the 1500s a monarchy was well established, with many kings coming from a noble Scottish family called the

---

You can see Viking Scotland at:

☞ The Orkney Museum in Kirkwall, where there is a boat burial which was found on the island of Sanday by a farmer walking on the beach after a terrible storm. Among the remains of the boat were three skeletons, swords, pieces of jewellery, a board game – and a Viking ironing board! The last of these is a large, flat piece of whalebone which a Viking woman would have used to smooth down her clothes.

You can see Scotland in the Middle Ages at:

☞ The island of Iona, where Scottish Christianity first began and a medieval abbey was built in the 1400s. You can walk down part of the medieval Street of the Dead which led from the abbey to the local village and wander over to the sacred royal burial ground where many kings are buried.

Stewarts. But all that stability was about to come to an end. There was a new religious movement called Protestantism which many thought should replace Catholicism, and they were prepared to go to great lengths to make sure it did. This period of change was called the Reformation. The queen, the very famous Mary, Queen of Scots, was Catholic. Mary found it hard to take control of her country. She offended the Scottish nobles by making a disastrous marriage (among many other things) and she was driven out of Scotland. Queen Elizabeth I was her cousin and a Protestant but she didn't want to help. She was so afraid that Mary would take over the throne that she had her imprisoned and then executed when a treasonous plot was discovered. Mary's son, James VI, inherited both the English and Scottish thrones, and so for the first time ever, England and Scotland were united under one ruler.

100 years later, in 1707, a law was passed known as the Act of Union, which stated that Scotland would be governed by a parliament in London. A

great many Scots were extremely unhappy about this and a
group of people called the Jacobites
plotted to bring back a proper
Scottish monarchy with the help of
Bonnie Prince Charlie who wanted
his family (the Stewarts) to rule
again – the fight with England
was on once more! But despite
rebellions in 1715 and 1745, they
didn't succeed and after a
disastrous battle on Culloden
Moor (between Nairn and
Inverness) in 1746, they had
to admit defeat.

By the mid-18th century,
Scotland seemed to have
changed very little: it was still a
poor, rural country ruled by a few
wealthy noble people. Countless
numbers of people from the
Highlands had emigrated to
Canada, New Zealand and
America to find a better life. And

24

although some left Scotland voluntarily, others had no choice. During this and the next century, many people were forced out of their homes by landowners during the 'Highland Clearances', to make way for sheep farming which brought in more money than rents from country tenants. Some landowners gave their tenants money to

emigrate or they built new communities for them, but others were ruthless and burned them out of their homes, or sent them penniless and starving to the towns to look for work.

The Clearances changed the face of the Highlands forever – thousands left, and the population has never been as large since. But those countries, especially America, that opened their doors to the Highlanders were given a great boost – the Scots were very welcome indeed because the population there was sparse. In the cities, things were changing, too. A group of scientists, inventors and philosophers – many from humble backgrounds – began to question the old ways of thinking. They wanted to understand the world properly and to improve it through

---

= *You can see Jacobite Scotland at:* =

☞ Glenfinnan, on the West Highland Railway near Fort William, where a huge column commemorates the arrival of Bonnie Prince Charlie at this spot, ready to raise an army to claim the Scottish throne.

☞ Dunvegan Castle on the Isle of Skye, where you can see a lock of Bonnie Prince Charlie's hair, preserved for more than 250 years.

science. They made many discoveries which were so important that for a long time Scotland led the world in the fields of medicine, geology, chemistry, engineering and architecture. This great period of thought and invention was called the Enlightenment.

Contrast all this learning and advancement with the tragic story of the village of Bettyhill on the northwest coast. Here, evicted tenants from the Clearances were reduced to living

=*You can see Enlightenment Scotland at:* =

☞ Charlotte Square in the New Town, Edinburgh, where an 18th-century house is open to the public. Many of the houses in this square have little upside-down cones attached to the wall. These are called 'link extinguishers' and were used by boys whose job was to escort people home in the dark by the light of a flaming torch. They would plunge the torch into the cone to extinguish it.

26

on the cliff, with children tethered by a rope to prevent them
falling off the edge.

Many of the discoveries made during the Enlightenment
were used to invent new machines to make the manufacturing
of goods quicker and easier. Hundreds of new factories
sprang up over Scotland, producing cotton, steel, iron and
many other things – and making them better than ever
before and faster than anyone else. Those people still left in
the countryside went to the cities to find work, which was
plentiful. This period of industrial expansion is known as the
Industrial Revolution.

It was now Glasgow's turn to play an important role in
Scotland's history, and during the Victorian age and early
20th century, it became one of the richest cities in the world.
Its factories made cotton, glass, paper and chemicals, engines
and trains, and on Glasgow's River Clyde, shipbuilding
became a huge industry. From 1870 until the start of the First
World War in 1914, Glasgow produced nearly a quarter of
the world's ships. The city of Dundee also flourished and
became known for its shipbuilding, whaling and the
manufacture of jute (a material used for making sacking and
rope). The port of Aberdeen expanded too – through fishing
and the shipping trade.

But not everybody was making money – thousands of
dock and factory workers often lived in terrible poverty.
   In the 20th century, Scotland began to get into economic
difficulties. The effects of two world wars and big changes in
coal mining, shipbuilding and other industries left many
people without jobs. Many Scots felt
that England didn't care about
them very much and wanted
Scotland to be governed by the
Scots. They even formed their own
political party called the Scottish
National Party, and in 1999, a
separate parliament for
Scotland was established,
the first for 300
years. The
Scottish Parliament
can pass some laws,
such as those on
Scottish education,
health, environment
and the arts, but the
British
Parliament in
London holds on
to the right to

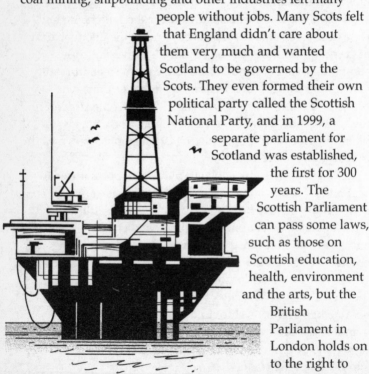

28

pass laws on those matters which affect the whole of Great Britain e.g. economy, defence and foreign affairs.

In the 21st century, the country is beginning to become prosperous again and in the past few decades new industries such as oil, electronics (Scotland manufactures nearly a quarter of Europe's computers and mobile phones) and tourism have sprung up to replace the old ones.

You can see modern Scotland in:

☞ The new Scottish Parliament building in Edinburgh. This is probably one of the most amazing buildings you'll have ever seen. It was designed by a Spanish architect called Enric Miralles and is very flamboyant and daring – it really doesn't look like a government building at all. Many Scottish artists were asked to create something for the interior, and you can see sculptures, paintings, woodcarvings and a fascinating tapestry with hidden messages in it. The building is very close to Holyroodhouse Palace and you can compare the old with the new. Which do you prefer?

Bonnie Scotland, Tartans, Clans, Kilts and Bagpipes

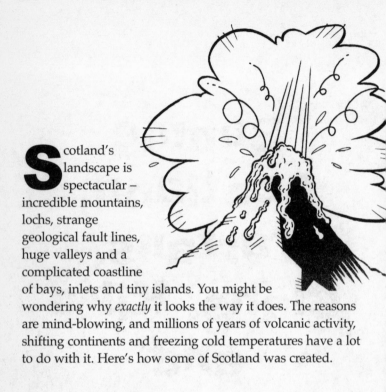

Scotland's landscape is spectacular – incredible mountains, lochs, strange geological fault lines, huge valleys and a complicated coastline of bays, inlets and tiny islands. You might be wondering why *exactly* it looks the way it does. The reasons are mind-blowing, and millions of years of volcanic activity, shifting continents and freezing cold temperatures have a lot to do with it. Here's how some of Scotland was created.

Bonnie Scotland

The Cairngorm Mountains

It's difficult to imagine, but 400 million years ago, Scotland and England were separate pieces of land 5,000 km (3,000 miles) apart. Eventually they drifted nearer and bang! they collided. Scotland crumpled, its crust buckled under the impact and great mountain ranges like the Cairngorms were formed.

The Great Glen

The collision created vast cracks known as fault lines and the most famous of these is the Great Glen, looking like a deep cut sliced through the earth by a knife. The Glen runs from Inverness on the east coast to Fort William on the west, a distance of 112 km (70 miles). It's so deep that it contains four lochs.

The other great fault line is the **Highland Boundary Fault**, which divides the Lowlands from the Highlands. If you're in the town of Callander, which lies on the Fault, look north and you've got steep hills and mountains; look south and the hills are more gentle. The village of Comrie which also lies on the Fault has had so many earthquake tremors that it has been nicknamed 'Shakin' Toon'. Earthquake readings are still taken at Earthquake House where the world's first seisometer was set up in 1874.

Arthur's Seat

350 million years ago in Edinburgh it was pretty hot. Several volcanoes burst into life, throwing lava and ash over a huge area. Arthur's Seat, a craggy hill that dominates Edinburgh's skyline at 823 ft, is one of those extinct volcanoes. And there are others in the city – Calton Hill, Castle Rock (on which Edinburgh Castle sits) and the lumpy hills in Holyrood Park.

Grey seals

The Ice Age brought grey seals to Scottish waters. When the ice melted, they stayed. Seal pups are still born with white fur – a legacy from thousands of years ago when snow and ice were everywhere and white would have been the best colour for camouflage. Not quite so necessary now!

Glens and lochs

Some 500,000 years ago the temperature dropped and Scotland was in the grip of an Ice Age. It looked and felt like the Arctic and the land was covered by a sheet of ice 1.5 km (1 mile) thick. Even Ben Nevis was buried beneath it. Huge glaciers were constantly on the move and, like bulldozers, they carved enormous holes in the landscape. Glens (valleys) that already existed were carved wider and deeper. These are known as U-shaped valleys because of the shape of them – a U not a V – like the U-shaped valley of Lairig Ghru in the Highlands.

Lochs were formed where the ice had gouged out very deep troughs. So when the ice that covered all of Scotland melted and ran into the sea, water remained behind in the lochs because they were so deep. It took 1,000 years for all the ice to melt.

The great pine forests

Pine forests cover huge areas of land in Scotland, but after the Ice Age, the whole of the country would have been *completely* covered by them. Many typical Scottish birds and animals, for example red deer, grouse and capercaillies (a type of bird) appeared around this time (11,000 years ago) to live in the forests. The Abernethy Forest in Tayside is a remnant of those ancient woods and will give you a good idea of what Scotland would have looked like before man came along and spoiled it all.

The west coast

This coastline is an extraordinary shape, wiggling in and out, creating hundreds of deep inlets. The land here has been worn away by the sea, by rivers and by melting ice and glaciers, leaving behind the many indentations that are typical of the west coast.

☞ If you want to know more about why Scotland looks the way it does, you should pay a visit to 'Our Dynamic Earth' in Edinburgh, a fabulous place that will tell you all about volcanoes, the Ice Age and how the Earth was formed. Look out for the earthquake simulator.

Tartans, clans, kilts and bagpipes

Tartan cloth was originally made in the Highlands from the wool of local sheep. It was tough, warm, waterproof and the colours came from plant dyes. The piece of tartan cloth itself was called a 'plaid' and was wound round the waist and over the shoulders, a little like a short toga. The colours of old tartans would have been quite dull, not bright like today's versions.

From before medieval times, people in the Highlands organized themselves into **clans** or tribes, led by a chief. All members bore the name of their chief, and each clan had its own special tartan pattern. The clans (more than 60 of them) were extremely powerful and ruled different territories in the north of Scotland for hundreds of years until the government took away their authority and most of their land in the 18th century. Clan chiefs still exist but they are now landowners, not great warriors.

Kilts are a more modern version of the 'plaid', normally worn with a sporran (a sort of pouch once made with badger skin, complete with badger's head), and minus the extra material that draped over the shoulders. Nowadays, Scottish men only wear kilts at weddings and other formal occasions, plus Highland Games, football and rugby matches. If you're a soldier, you'll be asked to wear your regiment's kilt at official army events. The kilt is a great symbol of Scotland and people are immensely proud to wear it. Properly made kilts cost hundreds of pounds, but you can rent them if you can't afford to buy your own. Women and girls wear tartan

The four largest clans are:

☞ **Stewart** Clan motto = 'Courage Grows Strong at a Wound'.

☞ **MacDonald** Clan motto = 'By Sea and By Land'.

☞ **Campbell** Clan motto = 'Do Not Forget'.

☞ **Murray** Clan motto = 'Furth Fortune and Fill the Fetters'.

How's this for two strange mottos? The MacEwan clan – 'I Grow Green' and the MacIntosh clan – 'Touch Not the Cat'!

too, woven into dresses and skirts. Some people say that you should only wear a tartan if you are from that particular clan – but most people ignore that.

Hundreds of years ago, **bagpipes** were played everywhere – in England and Europe, even Asia and were made from animal hide (skin). The Scots seemed to like them more than anyone else and they became the instrument of choice for getting the clansmen charged up for battle. The bagpipes are difficult to play: the bag has to be inflated by the blowpipe and squeezed all the time to keep the air flowing through the other pipes. Only one pipe, the chanter pipe, is used to play the tune. The piper is performing several tasks at once – pretty impressive!

A School Day in Scotland

Scotland was the first country in the world to pass a law – in 1696 – which said that every part of Scotland must have a school, and since then the Scots have been extremely proud of their schools and universities and their well-educated children. Scotland's educational system is separate from the rest of the United Kingdom and is a little different. Primary school begins at age four or five, depending when your birthday is, and continues until the age of twelve, when everyone then moves on to High School. In some of the isolated regions of Scotland, where numbers of pupils are often very low and the cost of building schools is too high, some don't change to a different school at all – they keep going to the same one. But maybe the teachers will treat them a little differently!

If you live on some of the more remote islands, then going to school can be a bit tricky. You might have to travel to another island and stay there all week, returning home at the weekends (if the weather lets you!). And where do you go for your school trips? One school solved this problem by setting up a video link to a museum on the mainland which provided them with some experts to answer the children's questions. Many island schools look out onto amazing scenery, full of wildlife, and studying their local environment is a very popular school activity. You might spend all day doing an otter survey – how cool is that?

If you live in a Gaelic-speaking area of Scotland, then you'll be taught in both Gaelic and English. Some Gaelic schools take part in a national televised quiz – all in Gaelic and quite a challenge.

At age 15 or 16, pupils sit exams in a wide range of subjects. These exams are called Standards. You're allowed to leave school after these exams if you don't want to study any longer, but if you do stay on, then it's only another year before another set of exams comes along – called Highers. And if you want to go to university, then there are more exams a year after that which are called Advanced Highers. Luckily, you'll probably only take two or three of these, and they're likely to be linked to the subject you've chosen to study at university. Now you can breathe a sigh of relief and go on a gap year like everybody else, but when you get back the university course is four years' long, not three, like the rest of the UK. Scotland doesn't get its reputation for being a well-educated country for nothing!

Food and Drink

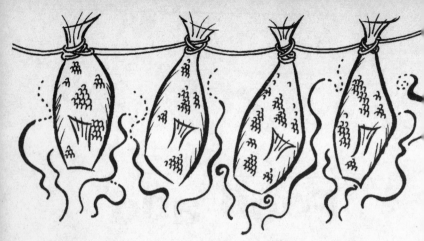

Scottish food has been strongly influenced by the country's climate and geography, so you'll find that many dishes are warming and filling (which will cheer you up after all that chilly weather). Potatoes and oats are staple foods because they grow easily in cold, damp weather, and the huge expanses of countryside and coastline provide plenty of wonderful wild food such as grouse, venison (deer) and countless varieties of fresh fish.

Here are some great dishes to look out for:

☞ **Arbroath smokies** – these are smoked haddocks from the fishing port of Arbroath on the northeast coast. They are often eaten for breakfast, sometimes for lunch, with hot, buttered bread, and are famous because of the special way they are smoked. You can see the smoking huts in Arbroath harbour, some of them are very old and date from the days around the 19th century when the fisherwomen would travel around the local area in their dark blue skirts and plaid shawls with their smokie basket on their back, hoping to sell them all.

☞ **Salmon** – Scotland is world-famous for its salmon. A great deal of it comes from the salmon farms around the coast but the most prized and, some say, the tastier, is the wild salmon, swimming free in Scotland's rivers.

☞ **Fish suppers** – fish (mainly haddock and cod) and chips! Found everywhere, especially on the coast, where the fish will be super-fresh, probably caught that same day. Have it with salt and vinegar or salt and sauce – a concoction of vinegar and brown sauce – an Edinburgh favourite.

☞ **Haggis** – the most famous of all Scottish dishes. It is made from the heart, liver and lungs of a sheep, mixed with oatmeal, onion and special seasoning, and stuffed into a sheep's intestine and sewn up! It is then cooked and served with neeps and tatties – that's turnips and potatoes. You won't find many Scots who make this dish regularly at home, though it's sometimes served as the main course at weddings and it can be bought at plenty of fish and chip shops – as haggis supper (haggis and chips). Don't be put off by the strange ingredients – everyone who tries it is always pleasantly surprised at how tasty it is. There's also a vegetarian version made from lentils, beans, nuts and vegetables.

☞ **Beef and lamb** – Scottish beef and lamb are some of the finest in the world. The lush grass of the countryside is very nutritious and makes the meat extremely tasty. Beef from Aberdeen Angus cattle is famous for its quality. Often served roasted with vegetables.

☞ **Porridge** – this is a very nourishing breakfast dish made from oats, and has been eaten in Scotland for centuries. People argue about the best way to cook porridge, so take your pick from: cooked with water and salt; cooked with milk and sugar; or cooked with milk, sugar, cream and a sprinkling of fruit on the top.

☞ **Oatcakes** – crisp, salty biscuits often eaten with cheese. You will also come across sweet ones made with sugar.

☞ **Bannocks** – oatcakes which contain some flour to make them softer, less crisp.

☞ **Cranachan** – a delicious pudding made from cream, raspberries, a kind of cottage cheese called 'crowdie', honey and plenty of toasted oats.

☞ **Skirlie** – oatmeal, onions, suet (a type of fat) and salt and pepper all fried together in a pan, and either eaten with potatoes and other vegetables, or you can stuff your chicken with it!

☞ **Scotch pies** and **bridies** – two different types of meat pie found in most of Scotland's bakeries, often eaten at lunchtime. Scotch pies are small and round, made from

44

pastry with a minced beef filling; bridies are a different shape, semi-circular and filled with mince and vegetables or onions.

☞ **Pheasant, grouse and venison** – roasted or in a meat casserole, served with vegetables. These meats are very healthy to eat because they don't contain much fat.

☞ **Scotch broth** and **cock-a leekie** – two soups to keep you warm. Scotch broth is made from lamb, barley and vegetables. Cock-a-leekie's main ingredients are – it's obvious really – chicken and leeks! Another lovely soup to look out for is **Cullen skink**, made from smoked haddock and potatoes.

☞ **Tatties** – potatoes, of course, but cooked in many different ways. Try **stovies**, a delicious dish of potatoes and onions, which sometimes also includes meat. And **rumbledethumps**, made with potatoes, of course, cabbage and cheese.

☞ **Raspberries, blueberries and tayberries** – the climate in Scotland is perfect for growing these soft fruits, and you'll find them in many dishes. They're often made into delicious jam sometimes flavoured with whisky (for grown-ups only!).

☞ **Shortbread** – this is a sweet biscuit, cut either into small rectangular slabs, or into a round, flat shape and then

divided into wedges, known as 'petticoat tails' – named after the ladies of the 16th-century royal court, whose petticoats the shape is said to resemble.

☞ **Tablet** – one of Scotland's most popular sweets. It's made from butter, sugar and milk, and is a little like fudge but not as chewy.

You might notice that Scotland has a lot of sweet shops selling sweets and *only* sweets. They're great shops, stacked with plenty of jars of what the Scots call 'hard boilings', sweets made from boiled sugar and flavourings. Look out for Berwick cockles, Moffat toffee, Hawick balls and Edinburgh rock.

☞ **Italian ice cream** – you will find delicious Italian ice cream all over Scotland – made by Italians! Confused? Well, don't be. There has been a large Italian population in Scotland right from the beginning of the 20th century, when many families left Italy to escape poverty. Many were heading further west to America, looking to travel on ships sailing from Glasgow, but some settled in

Scotland instead. They sold ice cream made from old family recipes, opened cafes and fish-and-chip shops, and this tradition is still maintained. Look out for wonderful Italian ice cream parlours, especially at the seaside.

☞ **Border tart** – a pastry tart, with a delicious filling of raisins and spice. Found all over the Borders region.

☞ **Selkirk bannock** – another speciality of the Borders, this time from the town of Selkirk. This is lovely, fruity bread, eaten with butter at tea time.

☞ **Black bun** – a little like Christmas pudding, but in a pastry case. Traditionally eaten at Hogmanay.

☞ **Irn-Bru** – the most popular fizzy drink in Scotland, and if you go out for a meal it'll be there on the menu. It's bright orange and tastes a bit like bubble-gum. When it first went on sale in 1901 it was called Iron-Brew but changed its name in 1946 to the spelling you see today. The recipe is a closely guarded secret, although we do know that it has a little bit of iron in it!

Some curious wee facts about

Scotland

According to Scottish custom, it's lucky if your first visitor on New Year's Day is a tall, dark man bringing a gift of a lump of coal. This is called 'first footing'

James IV became king of Scotland in 1488, at the age of 15. During his 25-year reign he became fluent in ten languages, and even practised as a dentist, charging patients for tooth extractions

The Forth Railway Bridge over the Firth of Forth is over a mile and a half long. It's made of 54,000 tons of steel held together by 8,000,000 rivets, and 57 workers died during its seven-year construction

Edinburgh author Arthur Conan Doyle, the creator of master detective Sherlock Holmes, believed in fairies. Holmes would not have approved!

Macbeth, the Scottish king about whom Shakespeare wrote his famous play, really did exist, reigning from 1040 to 1057. His full name was Mac Bethad mac Findláech

Och, bu' ah'm just plain Mac tae me pals!

Glasgow's Baloo Burger Company sells the world's biggest cheeseburger. It measures 18 inches across and weighs 10 pounds.

Scotland no longer has the death penalty for murder, but technically you can still be hanged for stealing a sheep there. So don't!

Fabulous Castles, Buildings and Sights

Castles

For hundreds of years, the Scots were almost permanently at war – with the Vikings, the Romans, the English or each other. It's no wonder, then, that the country is bursting with castles, more than 500 of them. You'll notice that there are many different designs, reflecting the fact that as weapons improved, castles had to become stronger and more sophisticated.

Duffus Castle, Morayshire

One of the oldest castles in Scotland, a 'motte-and-bailey' castle built in 1150 – an exciting new design in the 12th century. The motte was a huge mound of earth on which the main castle building stood, surrounded by a moat, while the bailey was an enclosed area on the other side of the moat where you would find the servants' buildings and stables. A bridge spanned the moat so you could get from one part of the castle to the other.

Dunnottar Castle, Aberdeenshire

A spectacular walled castle built on a huge rock, jutting out into the sea. Dunnottar has seen many bloodthirsty battles and sieges – and a daring adventure with Scotland's crown jewels. In 1651, Scotland was at war with England again and the crown jewels were taken to Dunnottar for safekeeping, just in time before the castle was besieged. The brave wife of the local church minister smuggled the jewels out in her apron and buried them in the churchyard until the coast was clear – nine years later!

Loch Leven Castle, Tayside

Loch Leven Castle stands in the middle of a loch and a small ferry boat will take you over the water to visit it. It is very isolated so it's no wonder that it was chosen as a suitable place to lock up Mary, Queen of Scots in 1567. She had been imprisoned there for nearly a year until 18-year-old William Douglas fell in love with her and helped her to escape. He rowed her ashore and threw the castle keys into the loch.

This castle is known as a 'tower house'. You won't see this design anywhere else in the world, but you'll see hundreds

of examples in Scotland. The tower-house design consists of a single huge tower divided into three or four floors, with very few windows, and battlements on the top. If extra room was needed, they built upwards. So some of them are very tall indeed.

Stirling Castle, Stirling

Stirling has seen a great deal of fighting – the sites of seven battlefields lie close by. The town is located between the Highlands and the Lowlands, so if somebody wanted to conquer the north of Scotland, they had to conquer Stirling first.

It's hard to imagine anyone attacking the castle because it stands so high and mighty on an enormous 80 m (250 ft) rock – but people did. The castle is very grand, with magnificent halls and battlements, reflecting the fact that many Scottish kings lived here, well protected and in great luxury. Look out for the courtyard known as the Lion's Den where one king kept his pet lion, and the kitchen which recreates the preparations for a great banquet for Mary, Queen of Scots. Have a good look at the Beheading Stone. Are you sure you can't see any bloodstains?

The Jacobite Steam Train, West Highlands

This train will take you on one of the most exciting railway journeys in the world, along part of the west coast from Fort William to Mallaig – the West Highland Railway. The train goes through mountain passes, crosses the amazing Caledonian Canal by way of a swing bridge, travels alongside a desolate loch and over the spectacular Glenfinnan Viaduct. The train and the viaduct have featured in three *Harry Potter* films, as has nearby Loch Shiel. Lots of local schoolchildren appeared as extras.

The Royal Mile, Edinburgh

This long, straight road – 1.6 km (1 mile) long, taking in four streets – in the middle of Edinburgh links the castle to the Palace of Holyroodhouse. Start at the castle, which towers over Edinburgh and is lit up at night. Look out for the motto over the gatehouse, *Me Impune Lacessit*, which roughly translated means 'No one messes with me and gets away with it'.

Further down the Royal Mile, there's a Camera Obscura where you can look at an amazing view of the city – through a Victorian lens and mirror, and it is projected on to a table. Carry on, and you'll notice the tall buildings and narrow alleys that run beside them. In the 17th century, Edinburgh was hemmed in by a huge wall and a loch (now drained), and so people had to build upwards. All along the Mile, there are shops, cafes and museums, including a Museum of Childhood, and the extraordinary modern and original Scottish Parliament building is at the end, opposite the Palace of Holyroodhouse.

Holyroodhouse is a royal palace, surrounded by a huge and quite wild park. Monarchs preferred this royal residence

to the draughty castle at the other end of the Royal Mile. Holyroodhouse is very grand with many ancient rooms, some of which were occupied by Mary, Queen of Scots. In the small room near her bedchamber, she saw her secretary stabbed to death in front of her very own eyes!

Skara Brae and Maes Howe, Orkney

On Orkney you will find two of the most amazing Stone Age sites in the world. **Skara Brae** is a 5,000-year-old village, preserved for centuries beneath the sand dunes. There are the remains of several houses, complete with stone furniture, including stone cupboards and beds! Elsewhere in Scotland, people would have used wood for furniture, but there are no trees on Orkney so poor old ancient man was left with little choice. **Maes Howe** is a huge burial tomb, so big in fact that you can walk into it. It's made from enormous slabs of stone, and has passageways and a central chamber where the bones of the ancestors would have been kept. Look out for the Viking graffiti, left behind when they raided the tomb looking for treasure, and if you're there at the winter solstice (21–22 December), then you'll have first-hand evidence of how clever the tomb builders were. On this day and this day only, the rays from the setting sun stream into the passageway and light up the inner chamber. Maybe these ancient people thought the sun would bring back their ancestors from the dead? There's a live webcam at www.maeshowe.co.uk, if you can't make the trip.

The Falkirk Wheel, Falkirk

The Falkirk Wheel has to be seen to be believed! It's a gigantic boat lift, completed in 2001, which scoops boats from one canal to another. Up until the 1930s, there were several locks which linked two canals, the Union and the Forth and Clyde, but they were filled in when people

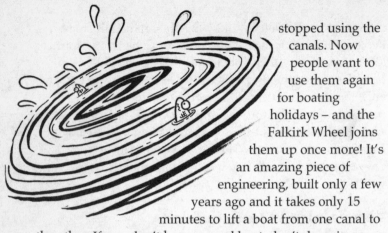

stopped using the canals. Now people want to use them again for boating holidays – and the Falkirk Wheel joins them up once more! It's an amazing piece of engineering, built only a few years ago and it takes only 15 minutes to lift a boat from one canal to the other. If you don't have a canal boat, don't despair – you can be scooped out of the water in a special excursion boat.

The Corryvreckan Whirlpool, near Jura

One of the three most dangerous whirlpools in the world lies just off the coast of Scotland near the island of Jura. It is a magnificent sight – swirling, bubbling water, great white waves up to 5 m (15 ft) high, and at times it is so ferocious that you can hear it from miles away. It once nearly claimed the life of George Orwell, the author of *Animal Farm*, when he was staying on the island and had gone out on a fishing trip. The Corryvreckan Whirlpool is best viewed from the safety of a BIG boat or from the clifftops of Jura in the spring when the tides are at their strongest. Don't get too close to the edge!!

The Northern Lights, anywhere in northern Scotland

Have you ever heard of the Northern Lights, also known as the Aurora Borealis? It would hardly be surprising if you haven't because they can only be seen in countries that are close to the Arctic Circle, and the nearer the Arctic Circle, the better. But Scotland isn't too far off, and if you're lucky in late September/early October or in February and March, then you might catch sight of them. They are streams of coloured lights – green, red, violet and blue – that appear in the night sky and appear to swirl around and move. It is a most fantastic sight, and although they seem a little eerie at first, there is nothing to be afraid of. It's all to do with the sun sending out clouds which when combined with gases in the Earth's atmosphere, give off these strange lights. They don't appear very often, so don't get too excited, but if you're lucky enough to catch them it's unforgettable!

Finnieston Crane, Glasgow

This magnificent crane stands by the River Clyde. When it was built in 1931, it was the largest in Europe at 59 m high (195 ft). Why so big? Well, its job was to lift locomotive railway engines – and they were pretty heavy! Glasgow was the biggest manufacturer of locomotives in Europe and from this quay by the river, they were sent all over the world. The crane would have lifted the engines from the quayside and on to the waiting boats. It is rarely used nowadays, but even so, it has become a famous Glasgow landmark and people often abseil down it for charity. Yikes.

Dryburgh Abbey, near Melrose

The ruins of this spectacular 12th-century abbey were once home to an order of monks famous for their extremely strict lifestyle. In the whole of the abbey, there was only one fireplace to warm them through the long Scottish winters. How hard is that?? Look out for the monks' night stairs, which they would use in the early hours of the morning on their way to the first prayers of the day.

The abbey is in a beautiful location by a river and surrounded by trees and hills. But life here was often far from tranquil: there are several accounts of fights between the monks, but that was nothing compared to what Edward II of England did. He burned the abbey to the ground after losing a battle.

If someone is giving you directions, they might mention the following:

☞ *tolbooth* = an old building once used as a prison and/or town hall. People would have paid their taxes (tolls) here at a booth. Old tolbooths have now been turned into all sorts of things, from shops to museums.

☞ *mercat cross* = a monument in the shape of a cross marking the site of the old market place.

☞ *kirk* = a church, and *kirkyard* = churchyard

Rosslyn Chapel, near Edinburgh

This amazing 15th-century church is made almost entirely from stone and everywhere you look, there are carvings of biblical scenes, of flowers, fruit, angels, stars and much more. One carving called the Apprentice Pillar has a fascinating story attached to it. It is a copy of a pillar in Rome and the chief mason was sent there to see it so he could get the carving right. When he returned, he found that his apprentice had finished the pillar in his absence – and it was perfect. He was so jealous that he killed him on the spot with a mallet. See if you can spot the carving of the chief mason, the apprentice with a wound on his forehead and the apprentice's grieving mother.

The Rosslyn Chapel has featured recently in a mega bestselling book called *The Da Vinci Code*, which you might have seen your parents reading. There is a theory that the Holy Grail is buried here in an underground vault. (The Holy Grail is the cup that Jesus drank from at the Last Supper.) It's a long story and some people believe it, some don't – but it all adds to the mystery of this strange church.

The Hollow Mountain, near Oban

Inside a hollowed-out mountain called Ben Cruachan is a
massive power station which uses the water from nearby
Loch Awe to generate electricity. The scenery round here is
so beautiful that it was decided to hide the power station
away so as not to spoil the view. You can take a ride inside
on a special electric bus to see the enormous cavern – the
size of a football pitch – where the giant turbines are kept.
It's just like being in a James Bond movie!

The Pineapple, near Falkirk

The Pineapple is probably Scotland's strangest building. It's
a 14 m (45 ft) high stone pineapple built for a joke in 1761 by
the local earl. It stands in the grounds of a stately home
where real pineapples were once grown in the Earl's
greenhouses. There are rooms inside and it's possible to rent
them for a holiday. That would be exciting enough but, in
addition, the surrounding gardens are home to great-crested
newts and a colony of bats.

The Forth Rail Bridge, North and South Queensferry

This spectacular Victorian railway bridge crosses a huge
estuary called the Firth of Forth. It took more than six years
to build, from 1883 to 1890, is 2.5 km (1.5 miles) long and
was one of the greatest achievements of the Victorian age.
The design of the bridge – called a cantilever bridge – was
very unusual for the time, and still looks unusual even now.
Eight million rivets hold it all together and 54,000 tons of
steel went into the making of it. The 4,000 men who built the
bridge were often in fear of their lives. 57 workers died in
accidents and many more had to be rescued by safety boats
positioned under the bridge. But pity the poor engine driver

who had to take the first train over. A few years earlier, there had been a terrible accident on a bridge over the River Tay which had been too weak to cope with the weight of the train, and hundreds of people had died. But he made it over.

Running alongside it is a more modern road bridge which is incredible too – but somehow the rail bridge beats it hands down!

Amazing fishing villages

The Scottish coast is jam-packed with beautiful fishing villages, but here are three very special ones:

Tobermory – this is a small town on the island of Mull. It's very jolly – brightly painted houses line the harbour, which is full of fishing boats. The children's TV series *Balamory* (shown all over Britain) is set here, and you might bump into the actors and camera crew filming in one of the yellow, blue or red houses.

Plockton – another picturesque village, which like Tobermory is full of gaily coloured cottages. It's famous for its palm trees which can grow here because of the west coast's mild climate.

East Neuk villages – lots of unusual villages with cobbled streets and little alleyways on this stretch of the east coast. Crail and Anstruther are just two of the ones to watch out for, and don't miss Lower Largo. This was the birthplace of the 'real' Robinson Crusoe, a navigator called Alexander Selkirk who lived alone on an island near Chile for four years. He wrote about his adventures in 1713, Daniel Defoe read them, and turned him into his novel *Robinson Crusoe*.

Glen Coe

Glen Coe is a spectacular mountain valley, famous throughout Scotland because it is so beautiful and wild. The mountains here are all very high (the highest is 1,050 m/3,465 ft), and are often covered in cloud, with waterfalls and hidden lochs. Walking and climbing in Glen Coe can be quite tricky and many mountaineers have lost their lives over the years, so perhaps it's best just to drive through and tick all the scary place names off the map – the Three Sisters (these are Glen Coe's highest mountains), the Devil's Staircase, the Study and the 'Lost Valley'. Don't take a wrong turning and go too far north – there's a Loch Hell up there!

Famous Scots, Great Inventors and Scientists

Two Heroes

William Wallace and Robert the Bruce are two of Scotland's greatest heroes and their achievements are celebrated nationwide. They both fought for the independence of their country and if they hadn't done so, Scotland would probably have just become part of England and not a country in its own right.

When **William Wallace** was born in 1270, life in Scotland was very dangerous indeed. There was no king, the land was full of English soldiers and the Scottish noblemen didn't care that ordinary people were being ill-treated. Wallace decided to take action. He rounded up a large army and they stormed castles, towns and cities until most of Scotland was liberated. In revenge, the English king sent a huge and very well-equipped army and Wallace rode to Stirling to do battle with it.

The 1297 Battle of Stirling Bridge is very famous, not just because the Scots won, but because this was the first time ever the English had been beaten by men with hardly any horses and armed only with spears. (They had clever tactics too!) Scotland was now free, and Wallace was knighted and made an important ruler. By the way, he was over 1.82 m (6 ft) tall, and must have towered over everybody: in those days, the average man only grew to be about 1.52 m (5 ft) tall.

But a few years later, things started to go wrong. Wallace fell out with the nobles and had to go into hiding. In 1305, he was captured and met a very grisly end indeed. He was taken to London and hung, drawn and quartered. The people of Scotland were devastated. He'd stood up for them when the noblemen couldn't be bothered and – unlike the nobles – he'd never done any dealings with the English. His death made the Scots more determined than ever to be free.

You can visit the Wallace Monument in Stirling. Climb the 246 steps to the top of the 67 m (220 ft) tower and gaze down over the famous battleground. Look out for Wallace's double-handed sword on display.

In 1306, a year after Wallace was captured, **Robert the Bruce** was crowned king. After Wallace's death, the English had taken charge of Scotland again, and Robert the Bruce decided he would have to set his country free before he could rule properly. The English king declared that he wouldn't rest until Bruce was dead, and so, with his family and followers, he went into hiding in the hills.

Even though Bruce and his supporters were living in caves in wild and lonely places, they still managed to gather enough men to capture castles and get rid of the English. But – like Wallace – Bruce had to win a very important battle before he could declare Scotland to be completely free. This famous battle was near Stirling at Bannockburn on 24 June 1314. The English army was the largest ever sent to Scotland, with nearly three times as many men as Bruce had. But

Bruce was a brilliant military leader: he got his men to dig huge pits in the earth and cover them with branches and turf to make them look like solid ground. When the English charged, the horses stumbled into the pits and the soldiers were stranded.

The Battle of Bannockburn was the greatest Scottish victory for centuries and led to independence from England for nearly 200 hundred years. When he died many years later, Robert the Bruce was buried in Dunfermline Abbey (although his heart was buried in Melrose Abbey) after the greatest funeral Scotland had ever seen. His tomb is magnificent and his name is written in huge stone letters around the church tower.

Charles Rennie Mackintosh

Charles Rennie Mackintosh was an architect and designer whose Glasgow buildings have become famous throughout the world. He was born in 1868 and was very interested in exciting ideas about design, especially a new style called Art Nouveau which was all the rage in Europe. He built several

buildings in Glasgow in this style including schools, churches, and a famous art school – and a very fashionable cafe called the Willow Tea Rooms. You can still pop in here for a cup of tea or a glass of Coke, although what you see is a reconstruction of the original interior. Mackintosh designed everything, from the menu card to the teaspoons to the strange chairs with high backs.

He built Hill House in Helensburgh for a Mr Blackie, a children's book publisher, and Mackintosh insisted on everything being either lilac or pink, including the servants' uniforms. One day when he came to visit he spotted a vase of daffodils that Mrs Blackie had brought into the house. Aaargh… yellow!! He demanded that they were taken away immediately, and Mrs Blackie was so embarrassed she blamed the maid.

Mary, Queen of Scots

Mary, Queen of Scots is probably the most well known and most romantic figure in Scottish history. Everywhere you go, you'll come across her name. Her story seems to capture everyone's imagination because it is so sad, full of drama and ends in terrible tragedy. Some say she was just unlucky, but others think that she behaved recklessly and made some crazy decisions.

She started out with a lot of bad luck which began almost from the moment she was born in 1542. Her father, King James V, died when she was just a few days old, and she was crowned queen. This left the nobles to quarrel over who should rule until Mary was old enough to do the job herself. It was decided that she should marry a French prince called Francis, and so when Mary was only five years old, she was separated from her mother and sent to France. When Francis finally became king, he ruled for only one year before he died. Poor Mary.

Aged 18, she returned to Scotland to rule her own country but more bad luck was in store for her. In her absence, Scotland had turned to the Protestant faith and, as Mary was a Catholic, that meant tricky times lay ahead. Also, she was a woman and had been brought up in France, so she didn't have a hope of understanding all the squabbling noblemen at the Scottish court.

What she should have done was behave sensibly and wait for things to die down, but she didn't... she made some very bad decisions instead. She married two terrible husbands one after the other: first, Lord Darnley, who brutally murdered one of her favourite courtiers right in front of her; and second, the Earl of Bothwell who had arranged for Darnley to be killed in an explosion. This last outrage was the final straw for the Scots and they imprisoned Mary and forced her to give up the throne. But nine months later, she managed to escape and instead of going to France where she would have been safe, she made her third bad decision and fled to England to seek help from her cousin Queen Elizabeth I. Elizabeth didn't want to help because she was terrified that Mary would stake a claim to the English throne, and she imprisoned her for the next 19 years in various English castles and great houses.

Did Mary take the safest course of action and just occupy herself with her embroidery and reading until Elizabeth realized that she was harmless? No, she didn't... she became involved in secret codes and letters and plots to murder Elizabeth, and was found out and beheaded for treason in 1587.

Her final round of bad luck was waiting for her at her execution – it took several blows to sever her head (the axeman should have done it in one), when the executioner picked up her head to show the crowd, it rolled away, leaving behind a wig! And then her pet dog crawled out from underneath her skirts, howling for his mistress.

She was a queen who had everything – great wealth and beauty (she was six foot tall) and had such charm that everyone she met fell in love with her, and yet despite that her life was full of disaster. Was she a victim of bad luck or a courageous person with a reckless heart?

Bonnie Prince Charlie

Bonnie Prince Charlie (he was called 'Bonnie' because he was very handsome) was born in 1720. His full name was Charles Edward Stewart and he was descended from an old line of Scottish kings who hadn't ruled for many years. Bonnie Prince Charlie thought it was time his family ruled Scotland again, and many others thought so too. In 1745, he rounded up an army of supporters and marched on Edinburgh and took control of the city. This conflict was known as the Jacobite Rebellion and there had been similar uprisings earlier in the century. They fought their way through Scotland, even captured parts of England, but were finally defeated by the English at the Battle of Culloden. It was a sad day for everyone who wanted the Stewarts to rule again. Had Bonnie Prince Charlie been brave or foolish?

There's a very famous story about how he escaped from Scotland. After the final battle, he was a wanted man and there was a huge reward if he was captured. When it looked as if he was about to be caught, he persuaded a young woman called Flora MacDonald to take him in a boat over to the island of Skye – and he would be in disguise as a young servant girl called Betty Burke. The plan worked brilliantly and he eventually fled to safety in France.

You can see Flora MacDonald's grave on Skye. She became so famous that hundreds of people attended her funeral and the procession was a mile-long. Bonnie Prince Charlie never returned to Scotland and was buried in Rome where he had lived for 22 years, dreaming of how he once nearly became king.

Walter Scott

Walter Scott was one of Scotland's greatest writers and you will come across his name a lot, especially in the Borders region where he lived when he was a boy in the 1770s. His grandfather had a farm there and Scott became fascinated by his relatives' tales of adventure and local life and legends – good material for his books!

His first novel, *Waverley*, was published under a different name, Jedediah Cleishbotham, because Scott was worried that people might not like it and he didn't want to be laughed at. But he needn't have been

☞ **Sean Connery** – This world-famous actor was born in Edinburgh. He first said 'The name's Bond, James Bond' in *Dr No* in 1962 (the very first Bond film), and went on to play Secret Agent 007 six more times. Many people think that he is the perfect Bond – tough, charming and a little mysterious. Before he became an actor, Sean Connery was in the Royal Navy. He acquired two tattoos: 'Mum and Dad' and 'Scotland Forever'.

☞ **Ewan McGregor** – an *extremely* famous film star. Recently played Obi-Wan Kenobi in *Star Wars,* but the first films he appeared in were set in Scotland.

☞ **Alex Ferguson** – This brilliant manager of Manchester United Football Club played for several Scottish clubs when he was a young man before he became manager of Aberdeen, who had not won a championship for over 20 years. Within a short space of time, they had won nine cups, including the European Cup Winners Cup, beating Real Madrid – and every team in the world wanted Alex Ferguson to be their manager and take them to the top.

☞ **David Coulthard** – top Formula One racing driver. He won several Scottish Karting championships when he was a young boy.

so concerned – it sold out in two days and he went on to write 26 more novels, including *Rob Roy* and *Ivanhoe*, and became extremely famous.

His novels were very unusual for the time: nobody had really written a historical novel before, and Scott loved writing about Scotland's past, especially about Bonnie Prince

Charlie and the Jacobites in the Highlands. His books were exciting, romantic and full of wonderful characters, and he inspired his readers in England (early tourists!) as well as Scotland to visit all the places mentioned in his novels.

Many of his books are still in print and Scottish children are taught about Scott at school. You can visit his house, Abbotsford, near Melrose, and you can't miss his monument in Edinburgh. It's 61 m (200 ft) high, very fancy and you can climb the internal staircase, stopping now and then at the viewing platforms to look out over the city.

Robert Burns

Robert Burns was a poet and songwriter whose most famous song is 'Auld Lang Syne', traditionally sung at New Year or Hogmanay, after the clocks have struck midnight. In 1786, when he was a young man, he nearly left Scotland to seek fame and fortune in Jamaica. He was waiting for his first poems to be published and he didn't think that anyone would be interested in them. However, they were a great success and Burns cancelled his trip abroad and became an overnight celebrity instead.

Burns was loved by everyone. He was witty and down-to-earth, had a rebellious streak and loved to poke fun at the wealthy upper classes. His poems were about ordinary people and ordinary things, and he wrote in the Scots language which everybody could understand. But unlike celebrities today, he didn't make much money and when he died aged only 37, he was still a poor man. However, there were more than 10,000 people at his funeral. He had fame, but no fortune.

Today in Scotland, Burns is a great national hero and his birthday (27 January) is celebrated all over the country as Burns Night when splendid haggis suppers are held. You'll see statues of Burns in many places in southern Scotland, especially around Ayr and Dumfries where he lived and worked.

David Livingstone

A remarkable Victorian explorer and hero who left his home in Blantyre to travel around Africa, tending the sick (he was a doctor) and exploring Africa's rivers and jungles. He made incredible journeys – one was 6,900 km (4,300 miles) long – and he mapped 2.5 million square km (1 million square miles) of what was then completely undiscovered Africa.

J.M. Barrie

The author of *Peter Pan* once said that he might not have been a children's writer if he had been taller (he was just over 1.52 m/5 ft). He felt happier in the company of people his own size – children! Barrie was born in Kirriemuir in 1860 and played for the local cricket team.

John Logie Baird

John Logie Baird invented the television – but it wasn't the first thing he tried his hand at. When he was a schoolboy, he set up a telephone exchange with three friends in his home town of Helensburgh but had to stop when a cab driver became entangled in the wires strung across the street and complained to his parents; and he once tried to make diamonds by using electricity and plunged a huge area of Glasgow into darkness!

Luckily for us he finally got round to inventing television. He'd first experimented with television when he was a teenager, and tried again as a young man but was so poor that he'd had to build a machine with whatever pieces he could afford, including pieces of coffin wood, a biscuit tin and a knitting needle. However, in 1925, he was so confident about his next television that he arranged to demonstrate it in a London department store. It was a great success and other inventors and businessmen stepped forward, eager to be involved with 'The Television Man', as he came to be known. After that, there was no looking back: two years later, the first TV picture sent over a long distance was transmitted between London and Glasgow; in 1929, the first television sets went on sale. By 1936, Baird's television company was broadcasting plays, operas, ballets and interviews with famous people. Baird was so dedicated to television that when he was taken very ill in 1945, he insisted on still taking charge of the televising of the victory parade at the end of the Second World War. From his sick bed!

James Hutton

James Hutton is known as the father of geology because he was the first person to realize how old the Earth is and to understand how it has formed over millions of years. He was born in 1726 and was always conducting chemical experiments, hunting for fossils and thinking about the scientific mysteries of the day. There was one particular puzzle he thought about a great deal – why are fossils of sea creatures found on top of Scottish mountains? Some people thought that this was because the Earth was once flooded, but Hutton disputed this. He worked out that the heat within the Earth had pushed up the mountains through the Earth's crust

– and so the fossils had risen up with the mountains. And that all of this had taken millions of years, not a few thousand, as some people thought.

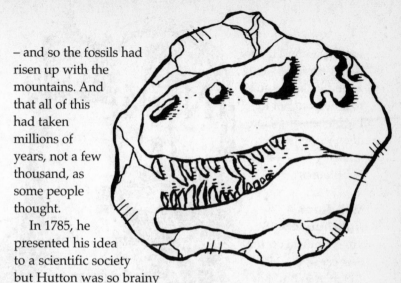

In 1785, he presented his idea to a scientific society but Hutton was so brainy that he was unable to express himself clearly and nobody knew what he was talking about. He wrote a very long book called *Theory of the Earth* but even when it was written down it still couldn't be understood. He really wasn't a very good writer! It was only when a friend wrote about Hutton's work that people finally realized that what he had discovered was very important indeed.

The Lighthouse Stevensons

In the early 19th century, four members of a family called the Stevensons designed and constructed 97 lighthouses on the Scottish coast, saving countless numbers of lives. It was an astonishing feat of engineering and brought great glory to Scotland and worldwide fame to the Stevensons.

The family, father Robert and his three sons, Alan, David and Thomas, were brilliant engineers who also designed roads, canals, railways and bridges, But lighthouses were their passion – the more difficult and dangerous to build, the better. Their greatest lighthouses were those out at sea, on rocks and reefs miles away from the mainland, lashed by hurricane-force gales and ice-cold seas. People said they would be impossible to build, but not for the Stevensons. Here are four of their amazing lighthouses:

Bell Rock lighthouse – 18 km (11 miles) off the east coast, it took 100 men to build it. Begun in 1807 and finished four years later. Bell Rock itself was completely covered by the sea at high tide, so the workmen had to make sure they got off in time as the waters rose.

Skerryvore lighthouse – 19 km (12 miles) out at sea in the Atlantic, built in 7 years, and said to be the world's most perfect and elegant lighthouse as it was so tall and slender. Skerryvore had no bathroom, just freshwater tanks for taking a dip in.

Muckle Flugga – the most northerly in Scotland, just off the island of Unst in the Shetlands. Next stop the Arctic Circle! The sea here was so ferocious that the men were constantly in fear of their lives.

Dubh Artach – this lighthouse stands on a 16 km (10-mile) long reef of rocks, 26 km (16 miles) off the west coast, built in 1872. This was Thomas's greatest achievement, and it was so strong it withstood an undersea earthquake two years later.

All the Stevenson lighthouses are still standing and in use, although they are now unmanned. You can visit one of them, Kinnaird Head lighthouse in Fraserburgh, preserved exactly as it was the day the last keeper left. Look out for the Northern Lighthouse Board plaque. This organization administered all Scottish lighthouses.

And another Stevenson

We haven't finished with this family yet. Its most famous member wasn't a lighthouse engineer, but a writer – Robert

Louis Stevenson, the author of the children's novel *Treasure Island*. He was the son of Thomas Stevenson, the builder of Dubh Artach lighthouse. Born in 1850, Robert Louis Stevenson nearly joined the family business, but he rebelled – he wanted to be a writer. He believed that, above all else, novels should be entertaining, and so it's no surprise that his two most popular books were an exciting adventure story (*Treasure Island*), the first of its kind ever written for children, and a gripping horror novel for adults, *The Strange Case of Dr Jekyll and Mr Hyde*.

Many of Stevenson's ideas for

81

☞ **Alexander Graham Bell** – the inventor of the telephone. The first words transmitted by telephone in 1876 were: 'Mr Watson, come here; I want you.'

☞ **James Watt** – Watt invented a steam engine in 1782 that worked so much quicker and efficiently than any engine invented before, and the industry and economy of the whole of Britain was completely transformed.

☞ **John Boyd Dunlop** – he invented the pneumatic tyre in 1888 and made travel quicker and more comfortable. He first used it on his son's bicycle.

☞ **Alexander Fleming** – he discovered penicillin in 1928 (which stops various nasty infections from spreading, and has saved many lives) and won the Nobel Prize.

☞ **Kirkpatrick Macmillan** – everyone who has a bicycle should be grateful to this man. Before Macmillan came along there were bicycles of sorts – penny-farthings and boneshakers – but they didn't really get you very far. Macmillan had the idea of adding pedals to power the bicycle from the back wheel, not the front. Now bicycles could go much faster, maybe too fast – he was once fined for reckless riding.

- ☞ **James Dewar** – this chemistry genius invented the thermos flask. Thank him next time you're enjoying a hot drink on top of a mountain!

- ☞ **Charles Macintosh** – almost by accident in 1836, he discovered a substance that made cloth waterproof. His macintoshes, lifebelts, boots, gloves and diving suits were in great demand in Scotland and all over the world.

- ☞ **John Hunter**, **James Simpson** and **Joseph Lister** were great pioneers of medicine. Hunter was an 18th-century surgeon whose knowledge of how the human body worked (gained by dissecting corpses!) transformed the medical world. Simpson developed antiseptics to use in operations to protect the patient from infection, and Lister promoted the use of chloroform as an anaesthetic, so you no longer had to suffer the agonies of an operation in the way people used to.

books were inspired by his travels round the Scottish coast with his family, looking at lighthouses. The map in *Treasure Island* which leads the hero to the buried gold is based on the island of Unst which Stevenson visited in 1869 with his father to look at the Muckle Flugga lighthouse, and *Kidnapped*, a children's novel set in the Highlands in the 18th century, features many places on the Scottish coast that were familiar to him. However, in *Dr Jekyll and Mr Hyde*, it was a well-known Edinburgh tale about a criminal called Deacon Brodie that inspired Stevenson to write a story about a man with two personalities, one good, one evil. It's one of the most famous novels in the world and has been made into a film 25 times!

Round the Islands

Scotland has a huge number of islands, 790 in total. Some are as much as 30 km (20 miles) long, some just a few metres wide. Only a small number of them are inhabited, and the rest are homes for puffins, seals and other wildlife. Some of the inhabited islands are close to the mainland and a short boat trip will take you there, but some are as much as 100 km (60 miles) out to sea and are wild and remote – no wonder some of the residents hardly ever leave.

Here's a quick island tour.

The Western Isles

The Western Isles are divided into five groups: the Outer Hebrides, the Inner Hebrides, the Small Isles, the Inner Isles and the Firth of Clyde Islands.

☞ There are no trees on many of the Western Isles. The rock on which some of these islands are founded is extremely hard (and very ancient – 3,000 million years-old) and it's difficult for vegetation to grow on it.

☞ The everyday language in the Hebridean Islands is Gaelic.

☞ At Barra Airport in the Outer Hebrides, the beach doubles up as the runway and planes can only land when the tide is out. Airport workers have to check that there aren't any stranded seals or dolphins in the way.

☞ Skye in the Inner Hebrides is the most visited of all the Western Isles, although Bute and Arran are popular too. Since 1995, a bridge has linked Skye to the mainland.

☞ Two of the Small Isles are called Rum and Eigg, and another one is called Muck!

☞ In the Inner Isles – on Jura – there is just one road, but Mull has a few more, just enough to hold a car rally every October.

☞ Bute and Arran are Firth of Clyde Islands. Bute is close to the mainland and Glaswegians have always come here for holidays. Its main town, Rothesay, is a Victorian seaside resort, with a pier. Arran is like Scotland in miniature, divided into Highlands and Lowlands.

☞ Because it's so difficult to get rid of things on an island, old and worn-out objects are often re-used in unusual ways. So don't be surprised if you see a clapped-out car being used as a chicken coop or an old bus just lying in a field, sheltering a few sheep.

The Northern Isles

The Northern Isles group is split into two – the Orkneys and Shetlands. These islands lie far off the north coast where the Atlantic Ocean meets the North Sea, and they are nearer to the Arctic Circle than they are to London. They're farther north than Moscow! They were conquered by the Vikings and many place names are in the old Viking/Northern Isles language known as Norn, and the number of archaeological sites – from Stone-Age villages to Viking boat burials – is amazing. And you'll find it doesn't feel like Scotland at all – people talk differently and think differently and you won't see a scrap of tartan, especially in Shetland.

- The main island of the Orkneys is called Orkney and the main Shetland island is called Shetland. Easy!

- Fishing, farming and oil are the main occupations. Deep-sea trawlers and oil supertankers can be seen – dropping off huge hauls of fish or filling up with oil to transport round the world. You can see the oil rigs out at sea, with their tall flares burning in the distance.

- The nearest mainland city is Bergen in Norway, and Norwegian is taught in some schools.

- It is said that a gale hits the Orkneys every 13 days.

- Like the Eskimos who have many different words for snow, Shetlanders have countless numbers of words for wind and rain.

- Nearly half of all visitors are from Scandinavia. They feel closely connected to these islands. Wonder why…

- In Orkney, a group of scientists examined the genetic make-up of the islanders. They found that one-third had Viking blood!

- In winter, there are only six hours of daylight but in the summer it never gets dark. You can read without using a light at midnight. There are a few hours when the sun goes down a little – this is known as the Simmer Dim.

- There are so few cars here that children don't know how dangerous they can be. A little road has been built in the grounds of one school so that its pupils can learn about road safety in case they ever go to the mainland.

Mysterious Scotland

There are more reports of ghosts and strange happenings in Scotland than in any other country – and nobody knows why. Maybe it has something to do with the fact that its ancient buildings have witnessed many gruesome and tragic events over the centuries. Here are some of the best stories:

Culloden Moor battlefield

Ghostly sightings were reported hundreds of years ago, just after this famous battle was fought in 1746, when people claimed to have seen the battle taking place all over again, fought by two phantom armies. But more recently it is said that you can sometimes see a lone, weary soldier in Highland dress, stumbling over the moorland. If you get near enough he can be heard to mutter 'Defeated.'

Britain's UFO hotspot

If you live in Bonnybridge near Falkirk, then you are in the best place in Britain to catch sight of one of the many UFOs that are reported to fly over the town. UFO spotters come from all over the world to try their luck. There have been some spectacular sightings here, not just the usual strange lights in the sky, but stories of shimmering discs appearing only metres away from people, video footage of a ball of

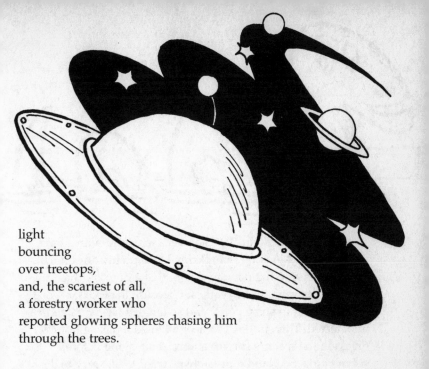

light
bouncing
over treetops,
and, the scariest of all,
a forestry worker who
reported glowing spheres chasing him
through the trees.

The haunted road

Take care if you are travelling down the A75 between Annan
and Gretna Green because this is Scotland's most haunted
road! There have been many unexplained sightings over the
years, including a man who suddenly appears in front of
your car and then vanishes, a lady in a cloud of mist and an
old lady who leaps into the road, running after a hen. By the
way, there's a ghostly car on Skye. All you see are headlights
coming towards you...

Loch Ness

Perhaps the most famous Scottish mystery of them all. Way
back in AD 565 there was a sighting of the Loch Ness
Monster, and there have been hundreds ever since. Many
claim to have seen the monster emerging from the water,
others have seen moving shapes on the loch's surface. A

famous photo taken in 1934, showed a creature with a long neck and head looking remarkably like a prehistoric animal. This gave rise to the popular theory that a dinosaur had survived for millions of years and because the loch is so deep (230 m/750 ft in some parts) and so large, it has remained undetected. Then in 1961, someone filmed a pair of humps breaking the water's surface and cruising along before submerging. So could it possibly be true? Well, sorry to dash your hopes but… The photo and the movie are almost certainly fakes, several hi-tech underwater surveys have failed to come up with any real evidence, and some scientists now believe that the monster might be a sturgeon, a fish found in very cold waters which can grow up to 6 m (20 ft) long.

But that doesn't mean that all experts have dismissed it completely. Nobody really knows what lurks at the bottom of Loch Ness and it's possible that there are deep caves and channels leading out to sea which would explain why the monster is so hard to detect. And very strange things have already been found, including a fish called the Arctic char, left behind from the last Ice Age. So, log on to the 24-hour webcam at www.lochness.co.uk and keep your eyes peeled.

A supermarket in Elgin

This ghost only appears at night when workers are busy stacking the shelves for the next day. Laughter can be heard, leaflets and paper suddenly fly into the air and sometimes a figure can be seen, wearing a cape.

Dunblane

In the 1970s many people on a housing estate in this town in Perthshire heard the sound of tramping feet as if an army was trooping past. Investigations revealed that in AD 117 the Roman 9th Hispana Legion had marched through Dunblane on the way to battle but later had disappeared without trace and never returned to their camp. The original Roman road ran directly behind the estate. Some people have also seen the lost legion itself up on the hills, trying to cross a river.

Sandwood Bay, north Highlands

This remote bay is said to be haunted by the ghost of a bearded sailor complete with sea boots, a cap and brass-buttoned tunic. Many sightings have been reported by fishermen, walkers and local people. He is thought to be a Polish seaman whose ship was wrecked in the bay hundreds of years

ago. And he may not be alone. Ancient local legends tell of mermaids swimming in the bay.

Underground Vaults, Edinburgh

Hundreds of people have given accounts of strange experiences in these ancient underground rooms beneath South Bridge in the centre of the city. In 2001, as part of the Edinburgh International Science Festival, a massive ghost-hunting experiment was set up which made it into *The Guinness Book of Records* as the biggest in the world. Over 250 people went down into the vaults and had to report back about what happened to them. Nearly half experienced strange smells, sounds, cold feelings and an unpleasant atmosphere. A few years ago a ghostly voice in gaelic was recorded, which loosely translated meant 'longing to go away', and that was very spooky indeed!

Go Wild!

Wildlife watching is really popular in Scotland because there is an amazing variety of birds and animals to see, some you won't find anywhere else in Britain.

Golden eagle and white-tailed sea eagle

These eagles live very high up in the mountainous, treeless areas of the Highlands, living on a diet of fish from lochs and from the sea and small mammals that roam the forest below. The golden eagle has a wingspan of up to 2 m (6 ft 6 in) and can be seen soaring above the moorland looking for prey. The white-tailed sea eagle is even bigger, making it the largest bird of prey in Britain – look out for them at Loch Awe. They're mostly brown with a white head and white tail feathers whereas the golden eagle isn't golden at all but a rich dark brown.

Osprey

Not quite as large and magnificent as the eagle, but big enough! Probably easier to spot because this bird of prey lives on lower ground. Look out for the osprey watch centres in Glentress Forest near Peebles and at the Loch of the Lowes nature reserve near Dunkeld and Abernethy Forest Reserve at Loch Garten where cameras observe their nests 24 hours a day. Don't bother in the winter though, because they fly to Africa for the warm weather, returning to the same nest in the spring to lay their eggs. You can watch the chicks being fed and trying out their wings.

Dolphins, whales and seals

Dolphins are found all around the Scottish coast especially in the waters of the Moray Firth (a huge bay on the east coast of the Highlands) where you can go on a dolphin-spotting boat trip. You can often see them from the shore, and at North Kessock there's a listening post where underwater phones allow you to eavesdrop on their clicks and whistles as they communicate with each other.

Several species of whale swim in Scottish waters particularly around the west coast near Skye and Mallaig. Killer whales, one of the fastest underwater animals, can be seen round Orkney.

Nearly half the world's seal population live around the Scottish coast. You're almost certain to see them… it would be hard not to with so many swimming around.

Otters

They're very shy and best spotted in the early morning and evening before the sun goes down, near calm water. A great area for otter watching is in the Highlands and islands, especially Shetland. Try your luck at Kylerhea on the Isle of Skye, or at Eilean Ban, a small island between the Isle of

Skye and the Kyle of Lochalsh, which was once the home of a famous naturalist called Gavin Maxwell. His best-selling book, *Ring of Bright Water*, was all about his life here observing the otters that lived close by. If your luck isn't in and you don't spot any otters, read the book instead!

Leaping Atlantic salmon

Don't be puzzled if you come across a salmon ladder. There's a very famous one at Pitlochry Dam and in spring and summer you might see at least 5,000 salmon using it. Atlantic Salmon are born in Scotland's rivers where they stay around for a while to grow, and then they swim downstream to the Atlantic Ocean. They spend at least four years at sea until they are full size, and then they make their way back to the river where they were hatched all those years ago. Scientists are baffled as to how they know the way. In many places on Scotland's rivers – only the ones that flow into the Atlantic though – stone steps (the salmon

98

ladders) with water flowing over them are built to enable the fish to get over obstacles such as dams. So go into one of the viewing chambers at Pitlochry and be amazed – where do those leaping salmon get their energy? They've already travelled 9,500 km (6,000 miles)!

Red deer

These are Britain's largest land mammals and most of them are found in Scotland. Autumn is the best time to see them when they gather together to find a mate, the males often picking fights with each other, but be sure to keep well away from them. Look out for deer in the Galloway Hills, on the Isle of Mull or in the Highlands of Perthshire. Don't trip over their huge antlers which they shed in the spring.

Wildcats

There are said to be only 100 of these creatures left in Scotland. If you ever wondered what cats might have looked like before people brought them into their homes and tamed them, then now's your chance. However, they are very rare and extremely shy, so don't be too hopeful. They live in the Highlands in moorlands and forests, and look like short, stocky tabby tomcats.

Highland cattle

All over the Highlands you'll see these extraordinary creatures (not just cows – bulls too!), one of the oldest breeds

in Scotland. You'll probably spot the reddish-brown ones first, but they come in black or white, too. They have extremely long horns, so long in fact that they have to have extra-long feeding troughs.

Red squirrels

This is a rare squirrel, once found all over Britain, now mainly found in Scotland. This is the squirrel that Beatrix Potter drew for her famous children's books. They're a lovely orangey-brown, with tufted ears and are very easily frightened, so don't make too much noise when you're out looking for them in woodlands in Speyside.

Whooper swans

These are not the everyday swans you see swimming around on ponds in parks. These swans are quite different and they don't normally live in Scotland at all but in Siberia and Greenland, and they come here in winter to warm up. You can see thousands of them at Caerlaverock nature reserve where the wardens feed them daily. It's quite a spectacle. Spot the ones that have just arrived from Siberia – they're too tired to feed and go straight to sleep.

A Little Bit of Sport

Football

Football is the most popular sport in Scotland. The country
has its own league and a Premier League of twelve of the
best clubs. One of two Glasgow teams, Celtic and Rangers,
win every season, and it's very unusual if they don't. There's
great rivalry between them and when they play each other
the crowds are massive and the atmosphere is very intense
and exciting. There's nothing to equal it over the border in
England, not even when Liverpool and Everton play. Both
clubs are amongst the top 20 richest clubs in the world, up
there with Real Madrid and Manchester United.

The national team (Scotland's team colours = dark blue
shirt and white shorts) play at Hampden Park in Glasgow.
You can go on a tour of this massive stadium and walk
through the players' tunnel, visit the changing rooms and
the football museum, and try out the machine which
measures the speed of your kick.

In the football season (August to May), matches are
played on Saturdays and sometimes Wednesdays. They're
generally good-natured and friendly, but be careful if you go
to a Rangers v Celtic match – they can get a little rowdy. If
you don't manage to see a game, you can watch *Scotsport* on
television instead, or listen to *Off the Ball* and *Sportsound* on
the radio or catch all the latest news in any newspaper, local
and national. Otherwise, just ask any Scotsman what the
score was – he's bound to know.

Rugby Union

Not as popular as football, but not far off! There are local clubs all over Scotland and Rugby Sevens is played here too, especially in the Borders region where this shortened version of the game was invented. Sevens is played with seven players instead of the usual fifteen, and each half of the game lasts only seven minutes.

The national rugby team (team colours = dark blue shirt and white shorts) play at Murrayfield Stadium in Edinburgh. Every year, Scotland takes part in the Six Nations tournament (held in February and March), and on days when these and other international matches are played, Murrayfield is a colourful sight with supporters lining the local streets, dressed in kilts.

Golf

One in 20 Scottish people play golf – that's more people than in any other country in the world. Maybe that's not such a surprising fact when you consider that golf was invented here in the 15th century, and there are public golf courses all over Scotland where anybody is allowed to play (in some countries, golf is an expensive and exclusive game – not so in Scotland). 500 years ago, there were so many men playing golf that it was banned. The king was worried that they were not practising their archery and he needed good archers to win his battles for him!

The town of St Andrews on the east coast is considered to be the home of golf. This is where the rules of the game were established by a group of players in 1744, and everybody had to stick to them. The players called themselves The Royal and Ancient Golf Club, and golf all over the world is still controlled by this club. There's a great putting course here which you can play on for about a £1. It's very lumpy and difficult – no wonder it's called the Himalayas!

Other famous courses are at Gleneagles, Carnoustie and Turnberry. When there's a major tournament on, don't be surprised at the massive crowds – people come from all over the world to see golf played in Scotland.

Mountain climbing

There are hundreds of mountains in Scotland, big and small, and climbing them is a hugely popular activity. Some of them are extremely difficult to conquer – many famous mountaineers who went on to climb in the Alps and the Himalayas did their training on Scottish mountains – but there are plenty of easy ones to try out. Many people take up 'Munro-bagging'. The Munros are a group of 284 mountains which are over 914 m (3,000 ft) and are named after Sir Hugh Munro, a president of the Scottish Mountaineering Club who first thought up the idea. The challenge is to climb them all and tick each one off the list as you go. It can take years! The first person to tick them all off was a vicar in

1930, and a few thousand people have done it since. The toughest one of all to climb is a 986 m (3,235 ft) mountain on Skye whose nickname is the 'Inaccessible Pinnacle' – its Scottish name is Sgurr Dearg, which means 'Red Mountain'.

Other outdoor sports include **trekking**, **running** (including running up mountains), **skiing** and **snowboarding** in the Cairngorm mountains, especially at Aviemore and in the Angus Glens. The snowfall can be a little unpredictable (that is, there might not be any) but if there is, it's a lovely place to ski. There are ski schools that will also teach you to cross-country ski across frozen lochs and there's a small railway near Loch Morlich that will take you up to the top of the slopes.

Hunting and fishing

Scotland's countryside is teeming with wildlife so it's no surprise that it is so famous for the traditional sports of hunting and fishing.

People come from all over the world to fish for salmon and trout in Scotland's rivers and lochs, and fishing hotels and schools are *very* big business. Some stretches of river are privately owned but there are lots open to everyone for a few pounds and a fishing permit. Sea fishing is also popular and there

will be plenty of charter boats in almost every harbour willing to take you out into the choppy waters.

Curling

Have you ever heard of this sport? It was Scotland's national game for 200 years until football came along in the late 1800s and knocked it off the top spot. It's a winter sport for cold climates and it is played on ice rinks, either outdoors or indoors. Curling is also played in north USA and Canada, thanks to those Scots who took the game with them when they emigrated there many years ago.

A curling team consists of four players: one of them slides a very heavy stone (nearly 20 kg/40lb) along the ice towards a target at the other end of the rink; another two players make it easier for the stone to slide along by sweeping the ice in front with brooms, and the fourth stands by the target, to speed the stone on its last few metres. The sweeping polishes the ice and warms it up slightly, making it easier for the stone to slide along. A complete match is made up of 10 ends, each end is 15 minutes long.

Curling is played all over Scotland, especially in the Highlands where you might catch a game on a winter evening at the ice rinks in Perth, Pitlochry or Inverness. It doesn't draw massive crowds but it is very popular, even more so after Scotland's Ladies' Curling Team won a gold medal at the Olympics in 2002.

Shinty

Shinty has been played in Scotland for hundreds of years, and is played nowhere else. It's a fast and furious cross between hockey and hurling. There are 35 shinty clubs, mainly in the Highlands, some of which have junior clubs too. You can catch shinty matches at many Highland Games events. The cup final is broadcast on national television and draws crowds of thousands of people.

Festivals and Traditions

The Scots are very fond of their traditions and love giving parties. They are renowned for their friendliness and hospitality, and you will be made to feel very welcome indeed.

Probably the biggest party of them all is held at **Hogmanay**, the Scottish New Year, celebrated on 31 December – and is usually a really lively occasion. In Edinburgh, Hogmanay has become an organized festival, and people come from all over the world to join in this party. It lasts three days, starting on 29 December with torchlight processions, dancing, piping and street theatre, and ends on New Year's Eve with a huge open-air concert in the city centre and fireworks at midnight from the castle battlements. And lots of kissing! Only Glasgow manages to have a party that is anything near as big (it has a pop concert with lots of famous singers and bands), but Hogmanay in Edinburgh is unbeatable.

In some places in Scotland, the New Year is celebrated with incredible ancient fire ceremonies.

Up-Helly-A, Lerwick, Shetland

This fire festival is said to be the biggest in the world and it takes place on the last Tuesday in January. Its strange name means 'end of the holidays'. For many hundreds of years, Vikings and Scots lived side by side in this part of Scotland, and at Up-Helly-A, you can clearly see the Viking influence.

The men of the town put on Viking dress – winged helmets, sheepskins, axes and shields – carry blazing torches and drag a replica Viking longship through the streets. At their destination, they throw their torches into the ship and watch it burn. It's an incredible sight. One man is chosen to be the top Viking and he must adopt a Viking name for the duration of the festival. Would you like to meet Olaf of the Sandals, Erik Bloodaxe Haraldson or Floki of the Ravens on a dark night?

Ancient Fireballs Ceremony, Stonehaven, near Aberdeen

At midnight the High Street is lit up with about 50 men, each swinging a fireball each on the end of a rope. It looks dangerous but don't worry, the fireballs (made of burning rags and twigs) are packed very tight in wire cages. Huge crowds line the street as the fireball swingers make their way down to the harbour and throw the fireballs into the sea.

Bonfire burning, Biggar, Borders

In the little town of Biggar a HUGE bonfire is built which burns for hours. Sometimes the townspeople get a bit carried

111

away – one year, the bonfire they built was so enormous that the fire brigade ordered them to dismantle it and make a smaller one!

Ba' Game, Kirkwall, Orkney (Christmas Day and New Year's Day)

In the streets of this town in Orkney, a strange ball game has been played for over 200 years. Two teams – the Uppies and the Doonies – must get a ball (the ba') into the other team's goal by whatever means possible – kicking, throwing or running with it. About 200 men play this game so it's quite a sight, and shops and houses have to board up their windows just in case. The goal for the Doonies is the sea.

Of course, many people stay at home for Hogmanay with family and friends. If so, at midnight, they mustn't forget to let in the 'first-footer'. This means that the 'first foot' of the New Year (the first person to come inside the house) must be a tall dark man carrying a lump of coal which he gives to you in exchange for some food, wine or whisky – or all three. And then everyone must sing *Auld Lang Syne*. It's a great tradition – very neighbourly and lots of fun.

Highland Games

Highland Games are staged all over Scotland in the summer months, and not just in the Highlands. At the Games, you will see some extraordinary contests known as 'the heavies' – tossing the caber (where men run with a massive tree trunk and throw it as far as they can), hammer throwing and putting (throwing) an enormous stone. Incredible strength and skill are needed to win. Competitions like this were first held hundreds of years ago so that Highland chiefs could pick the strongest men for their armies.

Just as important are the competitions for piping, Scottish

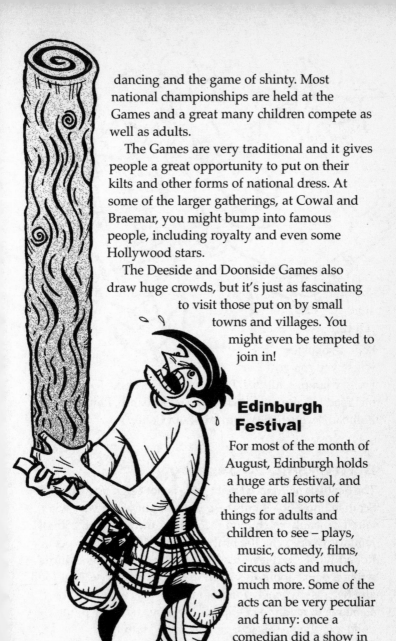

dancing and the game of shinty. Most national championships are held at the Games and a great many children compete as well as adults.

The Games are very traditional and it gives people a great opportunity to put on their kilts and other forms of national dress. At some of the larger gatherings, at Cowal and Braemar, you might bump into famous people, including royalty and even some Hollywood stars.

The Deeside and Doonside Games also draw huge crowds, but it's just as fascinating to visit those put on by small towns and villages. You might even be tempted to join in!

Edinburgh Festival

For most of the month of August, Edinburgh holds a huge arts festival, and there are all sorts of things for adults and children to see – plays, music, comedy, films, circus acts and much, much more. Some of the acts can be very peculiar and funny: once a comedian did a show in his red Ford Escort car – four people only! There's a

children's
book festival too
where you can go
and see famous authors. Previous authors at the festival have
included J. K. Rowling (who lives in Scotland), Phillip
Pullman, Jacqueline Wilson and Eoin Colfer.

Burns Night, 25 January

The Scottish national dish, haggis, is not eaten *very* often in
Scottish households but there is one night of the year when
you'll probably catch it on the menu – Burns Night, 25th of
January. Every year, the birthday of the 18th-century poet,
Robert Burns, is celebrated by the eating of a haggis. Burns
wrote a poem about this dish (in his day it was peasant food
and he was extremely fond of it!) and it is customary for
someone to read the poem aloud before suddenly plunging a
knife into the haggis in a very dramatic fashion.

Music and dance

There's a lot more to Scottish music than the sound of bagpipes – you might be pleased to hear! Traditional music comes in all shapes and sizes but the instruments that are used the most are: fiddles (violins), a small type of bagpipe, accordions and penny whistles. It's lovely music, sometimes jolly, sometimes sad, with songs about love gone wrong or a soldier killed in battle.

Over the last few years, lots of young Scottish musicians and singers have modernized traditional music and by adding different instruments, have made it more 'poppy' and very trendy. You can hear this 'fusion' of old and new at the Celtic Connections festival every January in Glasgow. But if it's pop music you really want to hear, then look out for the best rock and pop festival in Scotland called T in the Park. It's held in July near Kinross.

Music and dance come together at the ceilidh (pronounced 'kay-lee'). A ceilidh is great fun: the music is very fast and jolly, and you dance in a group, usually with a partner. The steps are fairly simple but there are plenty of them and a 'caller' shouts out the moves to you. A ceilidh is very informal, anyone can join in and they can be really exhausting. At the Riverside Club in Glasgow, a ceilidh has been held every week for the last 60 years.

Odds
and Ends

The mighty midge

The Highland midge is a tiny biting fly, and if you are in the west of Scotland during the summer and it's damp, cloudy and warm, then the midge and his 10 million little friends might drive you mad!! Scientists have tried over the years to find a way of getting rid of them altogether but nobody has succeeded – the climate in this part of the country is their ideal home. You can buy all sorts of lotions to spread on your skin that will help deter the midges, you can even look a bit silly in a special hat with a net attached, and lots of campsites and other outdoor places will help by using a giant 'midge magnet'. But beware: an old Highland punishment was to strip a person naked, tie them to a stake and leave them out all night for the midges. So whatever you do, don't fall out with your parents...

Missing bicycle

There's very little crime in Orkney. Once, the local newspaper reported a case that concerned a bicycle that had 'gone missing and could the person who took it by mistake please return it'. Hope they were reunited...

The young James Bond

Before James Bond became the world's greatest secret agent, he went to school in Edinburgh. James Bond is a fictional

The Desperate Dan statue in Dundee

character, of course, but the school – Fettes College – is real, and Bond's creator, Ian Fleming, describes his exploits there in the book *You Only Live Twice*. Originally, Bond was sent to school in England but was expelled and sent to Fettes College instead (his father was Scottish). As well as keeping up with his schoolwork, he did judo and boxing, kept out of trouble and left at the age of 17.

There is another Bond connection with Fettes College. Sean Connery, who played James Bond in many of the movies, was – among many other things – a milkman before he became a famous actor. And Fettes College was on his milk round. How amazing a coincidence is that?

The Dandy and *The Beano*

In the centre of Dundee, there are two statues that will surprise you. One is of Desperate Dan and the other of Minnie the Minx – characters from *The Dandy* comic. Just around the corner is the building where *The Dandy* and its sister comic *The Beano* have been produced since the 1930s by the firm DC Thomson. *The Dandy* came first in 1937 (you g a free whistle with issue number one) and *The Beano* followed on a year later. There have been a few changes since then: the 'Bash Street Kids' cartoon was once called 'When the Bell Rings'; and some characters have been dropped over the years, for example 'Tom Thumb' and 'Jimmy and His Magic Patch'. And you'd have to pay an awful lot more these days for that very first issue of *The Dandy* – £20,000!

The Screen Machine Mobile Cinema

In the Highlands and Islands, where the population is a little thin on the ground, there are very few cinemas. So if you fancy seeing the latest releases, and you live in the middle of nowhere, then you're a bit stuck. The solution? Let the cinema come to you! The Screen Machine Mobile Cinema is an enormous contraption carried around on the back of a juggernaut lorry which unfolds to provide a mini-cinema, seating about 100 people. It even has air-conditioning and surround-sound. It travels around the remote parts of Scotland, pitches up in a small town or village and stays three or four days. Only three people are needed to drive the lorry and set up the cinema, and ushers are recruited in the local villages. So, panic over, no need to miss the latest *Harry Potter* film after all!

An extraordinary island

The Shetland island of Foula definitely wants to be different. Way back in 1752, when a new calendar system was adopted in the rest of Britain, Foula dug its heels in and said no – and it never changed its mind. The island is still out of line with the rest of the country and celebrates Christmas Day on 6 January. By the way, it's a tiny place: it's only 5.6 km (3.5 miles) long and only 40 or so people live there, so maybe it doesn't matter very much at all that it's more than a week behind.

Emergency Phrases

Most people in Scotland speak English with a Scottish accent, but they will use plenty of words and phrases from another language called **Scots**. Words like these:

afore	before/in front of
auld	old
aye	yes
ba	ball (*fitba* = football)
bairn	child
bampot	stupid/silly person
breeks	trousers
burn	stream
ceilidh	a little party for dancing and singing
cludgie	the loo
coo	cow
dreich	dreary/tedious
heid	head
hen	used like this when addressing girls and women: 'Are you alright, hen?'
Mac/Mc	many Scottish surnames begin with Mac or Mc which is a Gaelic term meaning 'son of' e.g. MacDonald = son of Donald.
outwith	outside/beyond
peely-wally	someone who is pale and sickly. To feel peely-wally is to feel unwell.
tattie	potato
wee	small
wynd	a narrow lane

If you travel to the Western Isles, Skye or some of the Hebridean islands, you'll hear a completely different language called **Gaelic**. Gaelic doesn't sound anything like Scots or English, but don't worry – people will use English instead once they realize you don't understand. However, this language is used a great deal on road signs and on maps. Hundreds of years ago, Gaelic speakers used their language to name mountains, rivers, hills and other geographical features. Look out for these examples:

bam	white
ben/beinn	mountain (as in Ben Nevis)
corr	pointed
creag	a cliff or steep slope
dubh	black
dun	fort
eilean	island
glas	grey
glen/gleann	a valley with a river running through it
gorm	blue
loch	lake
maol	bald/bleak
meaell	round hill
mor/mhor	big/high

And on the outskirts of many towns and villages you will see a sign that says: 'Ceud Míle Fáilte', meaning 'A Hundred Thousand Welcomes'.

The only other language you're likely to come across is **Norn**, and this is only if you travel to Orkney or Shetland. Norn was once the language spoken here, and although it has now been replaced by Scots and English, some of the old words have been kept, especially (like Gaelic) on maps. The Orkney accent, by the way, is very soft and singsongy, quite unlike anything you'll hear in the rest of Scotland. Here are a few Norn map words:

ayre	beach
howe	mound
mool	headland
moorit	brown
mootie	tiny
muckle	large
voe	sea inlet

Good Books

Non-Fiction books

Visit Scotland, Anita Ganeri and Chris Oxlade, Heinemann 2004

The Story of Scotland, Richard Brassey and Stewart Ross, Orion 2004

Bloody Scotland, (Horrible History series), Terry Deary, Scholastic 1998

Ancient Scotland, Richard Dargie, Heinemann 2001

'45 Rising: The Diary of Euphemia Grant, Scotland 1745-46, Frances Mary Hendry, Scholastic 2001

Teach the Bairns to Cook: Traditional Scottish Recipes for Beginners, Gordon Baxter, Scottish Children's Press 1996

Scottish Castles Through History, Richard Dargie, Hodder Wayland 1998

Castles Map of Scotland, Collins 2005

Scottish Ghosts, Dane Love, Robert Hale 2001

Robert the Bruce, Barbara Rasmusen, Heinemann 1996

John Logie Baird, Mike Goldsmith, Hodder Wayland 2002

National Trust for Scotland Book of Scotland's Wildlife, Niall Benvie, Aurum Press 2004

The Bruce Trilogy (three novels about William Wallace and Robert the Bruce), Nigel Tranter,, Coronet 1985

McFootball: Great Scottish Heroes in the English Game, Norman Giller, Robson Books 2004

Scots Dictionary, Collins Gem 2005

Fiction

Treasure Island and *Kidnapped*, Robert Louis Stevenson, Pavilion 2003 and Puffin 1995. Great fun to listen to on audio.

Ring of Bright Water, Gavin Maxwell, Penguin (new edition) 2005

Oor Wullie and *The Broons* annuals, D.C. Thomson. A great way to pick up the Scottish dialect.

Silverfin (a novel about the young James Bond, partly set in Scotland), Charlie Higson, Puffin 2005

Look out for these contemporary Scottish children's writers: Julia Bertagna, Karen McCombie, Theresa Breslin (her novel *Remembrance* tells the story of a group of Scottish boys who join the army in the First World War) and Catherine MacPhail (in *Catch Us If You Can*, a boy and his grandfather go on the run in Scotland).

Wicked Websites

www.visitscotland.com
The Scottish Tourist Board website. It's packed with information about what to see and what to do, including several extras on food and geography.

www.undiscoveredscotland.co.uk
A great site with plenty of ideas about where to go, plus an online bookshop.

www.rampantscotland.com
A brilliant and mind-boggling site covering absolutely everything you ever needed to know about Scotland. You can find out about Scottish battles, haunted castles, sport, archaeology and plenty more, including a Where Am I? quiz.

www.scotsman.com
The website of one of Scotland's major newspapers. It carries

the lastest news and also has additional pieces about famous Scots, heritage and culture, myths and mysteries.

www.bbc.co.uk/scotland

What's on television and radio and fabulous in-depth pieces about Scottish history with great links to museums. Check out the wildlife section, too, which tells you where to spot birds and animals and has interviews with zoologists and wildlife experts.

www.ambaile.org.uk

All about Gaelic culture, language and music.

www.irn-bru.co.uk

Brilliant website about Scotland's popular fizzy drink.

www.stonepages.com/scotland

Everything you ever needed to know about Scotland's ancient stone circles and other archaeological sites. Full of great photographs.

www.bellrock.co.uk

All about the Bellrock lighthouse and the Stevenson family.

www.visit-fortwilliam.co.uk

Lots of information about Ben Nevis, the annual Ben Nevis race and bike trials. Also has a live webcam so you can watch the mountain all year round.

www.orkneyjar.com

Fantastic website about Orkney, its Viking history and what it's like to live there.

www.scotprem.com

The website of Scotland's Premier Football league.

www.scottishrugby.org

All the latest news and fixtures.

www.scotlandspeople.gov.uk

If you think you might have Scottish ancestors and you want

to trace your family tree, then this is a good place to start.

www.hogmanay.net

Tells you all about the tradition of Hogmanay and where to find the best fire festivals, bonfires and parties.

www.sciencefestival.co.uk

All the events at Edinburgh's annual science festival.

www.tinthepark.com

Who's appearing at the next festival and how to buy tickets. Has a great photo gallery of all the bands and singers who have appeared since it began ten years ago.

www.musicinscotland.com

All about traditional music and where to catch live events.

www.thatsbraw.co.uk

Great website about two famous Scottish newspaper cartoon strips – *Oor Wullie* and *The Broons*. It tells you all about the characters and the cartoonists who first drew them. Also has some good screensavers.